The Well-Adjusted Child

The Social Benefits of Homeschooling

RACHEL GATHERCOLE

Mapletree Publishing Company
Denver, Colorado

Printed in the United States of America
12 11 10 09 08 07   1 2 3 4 5 6 7

Cover design by Tamara Dever   www.tlcgraphics.com

Library of Congress Cataloging-in-Publication Data

Gathercole, Rachel, 1973-
   The well-adjusted child : the social benefits of
homeschooling / by Rachel Gathercole.
       p. cm.
   Includes bibliographical references.
   ISBN-13: 978-1-60065-107-6 (alk. paper)
   ISBN-10: 1-60065-107-0 (alk. paper)
 1. Home schooling—Social aspects. 2. Socialization.
I. Title.
LC40.G38 2007
371.04'2—dc22

                                        2006036721
                                             CIP

Excerpts from *Family Matters, Why Homeschooling Makes Sense,* ©1992
by David Guterson, reprinted by permission of Harcourt, Inc.

Printed on acid-free paper

Mapletree Publishing Company
Denver, Colorado 80130
800-537-0414
www.mapletreepublishing.com
The Mapletree logo is a trademark of Mapletree
Publishing Company

This book is dedicated to the women, men, and children of THEA, most especially Zach, Saul, Sadie, and Luke.

"There's a land that I see where the children are free,
And I say it ain't far to this land from where we are.
Take my hand, come with me, where the children are free;
Come with me, take my hand, and we'll live
In a land where the river runs free
In a land through the green country
In a land to a shining sea
Where you and me are free to be
You and me."

Marlo Thomas
Free To Be You and Me

Used with permission from The Free To Be Foundation, Inc.

TABLE OF CONTENTS

FOREWORD

"What about socialization?" That question provokes a subdued, almost rote, response from me now that I've worked with homeschoolers for twenty-five years. Probably the hardest thing about being a homeschooler is repeatedly answering questions about homeschooling and socialization. Often these questions are honest exchanges, but sometimes they implicitly carry a criticism: "Aren't you socially handicapping your child by homeschooling them?" It is hard to feel good about discussing homeschooling with someone who seems to assume that by keeping your family close you are automatically suffocating them. Further, a tactful reply is not always easy when you are fielding questions from folks who already have their answers.

However, the last thing I have ever been worried about as a homeschooling father of three daughters is their socialization. Homeschooling has always allowed them lots of time and opportunities to make and sustain friendships with children and adults. In fact, now that my girls are young adults and teenagers I'm more comfortable than ever with our decision to homeschool our children. All the risks we were warned about when we homeschooled our girls turned out to be stale conventional wisdom: they won't learn anything, they'll be put in lower level classes if they return to school, they won't be able to get into college or find work, especically—*they won't be socialized!*

Now, homeschooling isn't the answer to everything, and not everyone should homeschool. Homeschooling is and should remain a self-selecting and self-correcting activity. But, given the amount of books, articles, movies, videos, plays, and personal stories about the everyday de-socializing experiences children experience in the course of contemporary schooling, I am amazed how people think this type of socialization is the best we can offer children. "It's the real world," is a sad, and wrong, response. Bullying, verbal and emotional abuse, forced labor and stress from one's workload at least have some hope of remedy or adjudication in the real world of adult work. In the world of school socialization, these are just things kids must get used to. "After all," supporters of school socialization contend, "Our kids need to be citizens in a democracy..." Well, now I think we're really on thin ice. As a homeschooling mother wrote to a school official in 1921: How can democracy be taught in an institution that doesn't practice it? But I digress...

Socialization. With all the tension in our world from differing political views, differing religious views, and differing classes, we can certainly use better social skills and socialization. However, school is increasingly becoming a place where testing and competition are paramount virtues, not individually-paced learning and group cooperation. Our children need other social outlets besides the increasingly limited opportunities schools provide, and it is homeschoolers who are finding or creating many new opportunities for children and adults to socialize during "school hours." It will be a sad irony that homeschoolers may someday soon be criticized for allowing their children to be so social that they might fall behind their schooled age-mates who are compelled to spend so much more of their "time on task!"

That is one reason why Rachel Gathercole's book appeals to me: she presents data, stories, and research about how homeschoolers develop social skills and, in doing so, she demonstrates the wide variety of possibilities for socializing children that exist in the real world besides sending them to school. The other reason I like this book is that the next time someone says to me, "I'm thinking about homeschooling but I worry that my child won't be properly socialized," I can just hand them this book.

Patrick Farenga
Co-author of *Teach Your Own: The John Holt Book of Homeschooling*
President of Holt Associates, Inc.
Former publisher of
Growing Without Schooling magazine

PREFACE

Why This Book?

If there were a prize for the most misunderstood aspect of homeschooling, socialization would surely be the blue ribbon winner.

When I first stumbled upon homeschooling, I had the same images of it as most people do. A staunch supporter of public education, I had concerns about homeschooling—particularly about socialization—that were both many and typical. It was not until I became a homeschooler myself that I began to glimpse the true realities of homeschooling.

Today I have been a homeschooling parent for ten years. Though, like all aspects of parenting, it has its challenges, homeschooling has proven to be a wonderful experience for me and my family. I believe I can honestly say there is nothing my family and I don't like about it. In fact, we feel tremendously lucky to have landed, somehow, on this path-off-the-beaten-path.

But I didn't always know it would be this way. For me, the road to homeschooling was a long and educational one, and the final destination was not at all what I expected.

My days as a public school child had two faces. Always an "A" student and often a teacher's pet, I seemed academically a success. Socially, my school life was much less predictable. I was, at turns, a "normal" child, a complete reject, a nerd, a geek, a popular kid, a safety patrol, and an "invisible" child. One early report card noted that I "socialized too much," while a later one from a different school commented that I "chose" to isolate myself from the other children. As the years went on and I gradually figured out how to maneuver socially in school, I discovered that when I was socially successful, it detracted from my academic success, and when I was academically focused, I had difficulty socially. More importantly, I found that, at least in that environment, being myself was never enough; I had to "figure out" how to act to have friends, and a lot of that involved pretending I wasn't as smart or articulate as I was, pretending I didn't care about school, and often dressing in certain clothes and wearing my hair in certain ways. I discovered that although my family did not have money for expensive clothes, I could bluff a little bit by wearing certain things that at least suggested current styles. But never was being myself a helpful social activity, until the end of high school when my popularity was already established, and even then it was probably largely because I was attending a very unique arts school that lacked typical high school social structures.

Despite all that, I loved school. Throughout my childhood I attended exceptionally good schools, including magnet schools, and enjoyed getting up each morning and looked forward to arriving at school each day. By high school I had finally learned to navigate the social system. By graduation I somehow managed to rank third in my class with an "A" average. I was also president of both the National Honor Society and the Key Club (a service club), surrounded by lots of friends, and dating a very nice guy who also happened to be one of the most popular guys in school. The price I paid for this brief glory was a childhood of "faking it," pretending to be what I was not.

Perhaps this sounds like a success story. A good experience in which I learned the social ropes that one is supposed to learn in school. This is what adolescence, at least, is all about, isn't it? Learning to "fit in" to school life and thus to society. So I thought—until I discovered homeschooling.

The experience of going to school is one most of us understand and share. It is so ingrained in our culture that we barely distinguish school-going from childhood itself. There is little I could tell you about school that has not been said a hundred times by other authors and probably by you yourself in conversation.

But in the experience of homeschooling I have discovered a completely new world of information, experience, and perspectives largely unknown to the majority of Americans. I have spoken to hundreds of other homeschoolers, read dozens of books and articles by experts on the subject, and observed the fascinating day-to-day lives of my own children and their many homeschooled peers. The experience of homeschooling, I have found, is a misunderstood one, completely different from that which the public at large imagines, and one that is becoming increasingly common and important to understand. It is this experience, and the hidden truths about it, that I seek to share with you in this book.

Every day I see people worry about homeschoolers' socialization, just as I once did. I see people right and left choose not to homeschool, solely because of a vague sense that their children (or they themselves) will not have adequate social opportunities. They believe that they and their children will be stuck at home, friendless, weird. They have no idea that, at that very moment, droves of homeschooled children are playing at the park together, sleeping over at each other's houses, and taking classes together. Homeschooling parents are gathering for picnics, brunches, game nights at each other's houses, and so on. The concerned parents miss out on the many benefits of homeschooling—including the ones that drew them to consider homeschooling in the first place—in the name of socialization, never knowing that homeschooling offers not only academic and other important benefits, but social benefits as well. Some parents who do choose to homeschool also worry about socialization, perhaps in some cases because they are not aware that right in their communities there are other homeschoolers whom they can connect with. The idea that homeschoolers lack social opportunities is simply not supported by fact. In truth, many homeschoolers find that the social life is one of the primary benefits of homeschooling for them.

Parents today want very much to choose the best path for their children—there is no doubt of that. But the information available on which to base these decisions has thus far been sadly incomplete.

This book will close that gap and provide real information about socialization and the social lives homeschoolers lead so that you can see for yourself the kind of social life that homeschooling really offers.

If you are a parent considering homeschooling, this book will give you the valuable information and support that you need to make a truly informed choice about your children's education. If you are already homeschooling, or are the relative or friend of a homeschooler, it will give you support and information you need in order to relax in the knowledge that the homeschooled children in your life are benefiting socially as well as academically from homeschooling.

Be warned, though: the purpose of this book is not to prove that all homeschoolers are well socialized. The purpose is to share the opinions, experiences, perspectives, and thoughts of some homeschoolers and to show through these experiences the opportunities and benefits that homeschooling can offer for good socialization.

This book will not claim that there is no such thing as a "bad apple" parent who does not take advantage of these opportunities and benefits for their children any more than it will suggest that there are no "bad apple" parents whose children attend school. That's okay. If you are not a "bad apple," then you needn't worry that your children will suffer socially if homeschooled. It also will not claim that homeschoolers are in some way "better" than conventional schoolers, or vice versa.

This book will simply show how and why a great many homeschoolers are reaping enormous social benefits from homeschooling. If you are a person who is considering homeschooling, or is already homeschooling, this book will show how and why your child can enjoy those benefits through homeschooling, too.

Understanding the realities of homeschool socialization will relieve your worries about homeschoolers and allow you to effectively address your children's social needs without fear or to support and discuss in an informed manner your friends' or relatives' choice to homeschool. Freedom from unnecessary worry about socialization allows families to have more enjoyable and productive times together. And when we understand homeschooling and socialization clearly from the perspective of those who see it happen on a day-to-day basis, concerns about homeschool socialization can simply melt away.

We all want to be close to our families. Parents want to get along with their kids. Kids want to be close to their parents. Grandparents want to support their grandchildren. Millions of parents are choosing homeschooling because of the many, many benefits it offers to children and families. With the knowledge that socialization is one of these benefits, we can have the freedom to more deeply enjoy our children, our grandchildren, and our lives.

As it always does, "The truth shall make you free."

ACKNOWLEDGMENTS

Just as it takes a village to raise a child, so does it take a village to write and publish a book. In the long, edifying process of creating this book, there have been a number of people whose help and support has been invaluable to me. I would like to offer my humble appreciation to each of them. Specifically, I would like to thank:

All of the men, women, and children who generously gave of their time and energy to share their stories, thoughts, and experiences with me. You are the heart and soul of this book. I cannot mention your names here, for privacy reasons, but you know who you are.

My publisher, David Hall, for believing in me and this project and for recognizing the need for this book.

My editor, Lacey Klingler, for her careful work and helpful advice.

My agent, Sheree Bykofsky and her associate Janet Rosen, for their support and assistance.

Thom Loubet and the Free To Be Foundation, Inc., for their flexibility and generosity in allowing me to quote a large excerpt from the song "Free to Be... You and Me."

Mirtha Estrada, steadfast and cherished friend, for taking the time to read and give insightful feedback and encouragement on this book early in the process.

All the friends, relatives, and strangers, who, through their curious questions and heartfelt concerns, repeatedly reminded me of the need for this book. It is you who kept me returning to the keyboard night after night while my children slept.

Kim Pickett, wherever you are, for giving me my first fateful glimpse of homeschooling.

Professor Joe Viscomi, who, in what may have been the most formative moment of my academic career, unknowingly inspired all my future writing efforts when he casually said to me: "If you can articulate something that is obvious to you, you've done us all a favor."

The authors of the many great books and articles I have quoted or listed in the bibliography, who have shaped my life as well as the content of this book.

The faculty and class of 1991 of the New World School of the Arts, for giving me both a truly fantastic high school experience and the knowledge that teenagers are far more than their culture makes them out to be.

The women, men, and children of THEA, my companions on this long, educational journey. You are my friends, my teachers, my mentors, my loved ones, my home away from home. This book could not exist without you. I am honored and humbled to know each of you. I am especially indebted to Annie Collins, Christine Davis, Sarah Howe, Libby Searles-Bohs, Kristie Wells, Sally Freeman, Rachel Mehalek, and Jim and Cathy Chickos, for their wisdom, modeling, and years of support and inspiration in the areas of child-rearing and education. In addition, I am very grateful to:

Jenny Warnasch for both her friendship and her careful reading and insightful suggestions relating to the text;

Alicia Best and Lucinda Robinson, for being people I really could truly trust with my kids while I wrote;

And Corrin Fleming—you have been a source of inspiration to me for the last eight years. You are brilliant, beautiful, kind, fun to be around, and incredibly talented. Don't ever let anyone tell you otherwise.

And finally, I would like to give my most heartfelt thanks to:

My parents, Virginia Mueller and Geoffrey Gathercole, for teaching me to think independently and to question, and for telling me repeatedly that I could do anything I wanted to do;

Saul, Sadie, and Luke, my muses, for challenging and inspiring me, for giving me something worthwhile to write about, and for making my life more meaningful and wonderful than I ever thought a life could be;

And Zach, for years of open-minded, faithful support and loving partnership in raising and educating our children; and for providing constant encouragement, countless hours of writing time, a reliable sounding board, and brilliant insights and feedback related to the writing of this book. In so many ways you have made all of this possible. Thank you.

INTRODUCTION

A STORY

O nce upon a time, all children were homeschooled. They were not sent away from home each day to a place just for children but lived, learned, worked, and played in the real world, alongside adults and other children of all ages. They admired the adults, many of whom acted as wise helpers, protectors, and friends to the children. By living and learning in the real world, they learned to interact with people of all ages. Also, through observing the adults in their community going about their lives on a daily basis, they learned, in time, what was expected of people in their culture, what behaviors were accepted and effective, what qualities were valued and useful, and ultimately, how to be successful adults. This didn't require a lot of effort, though; they learned all this automatically because, as children, they were naturally driven to do so. As members of a social species, they learned to fit into their culture as effortlessly and naturally as they breathed and slept.

Children, on the whole, have grown up into functional adults this way since the beginning of the human race, bringing us almost all the way to where we are today. Then one day about two hundred years ago, along came compulsory schooling. For various reasons, children began to spend their days in schools, where they were grouped by age and their social contact was limited to short stints during the day, during which they were able to interact briefly with peers their own age and adults who were forced by their circumstances to act as disciplinarians or instructors and little more. Still, this grouping was necessary because the schools were charged with the task of educating large numbers of children at once, using a very limited number of adults. Therefore, children *had* to be grouped roughly according to age so that material could be taught in a standardized rather than an individualized manner. The placing of same-age peers together in large groups (without other-aged children and adults), while unnatural, was a convenience and a pragmatic necessity.

Over the years, school took up more and more time and eventually became such a huge part of childhood that school life came to be viewed as synonymous with childhood itself. People forgot that there had ever been life without chalkboards, desks, and recess and could not imagine childhood without it. All children were students. All friends were located within the schoolhouse walls. Being around large groups of peers was seen as not a convenience but an important and necessary part of growing up. Quite simply, school was childhood, and childhood was school.

By and by, a separate culture began to develop—a school culture. Children began to learn certain behaviors (some of them unhealthy) in order to get on in this ever-stranger environment in which, for the first time, the children had to fend largely for themselves. These behaviors included teasing, competitiveness, peer dependence, expressing a disdain for adults, excessive concerns about appearance and "sameness" with others, and so on. Soon these, too, came to be seen as normal—

even necessary—traits for all children. A child who did not exhibit these characteristics would soon come to be viewed as abnormal. It was like an epidemic of pox that had spread to all members of a society and stayed so long that people forgot what it was like before the red spots and viewed people without them as freaks. Although people commonly complained about a growing "generation gap," the failings of school systems, the deterioration of values among youths, violence in schools, and so on, still many people came to believe that it was *necessary* and inherently appropriate that children be in this environment and exhibit these behaviors. Eventually, it came to be thought that school, in spite of its failings, was the *one right place* for children to grow up and become socialized. Any other environment was, by default, barren, empty, unhealthy, and sad.

Still, a few people felt in their gut that their children didn't belong there. And thus came homeschoolers. One by one, they said, "I think kids don't *have* to go to school to learn or be healthy. I think my kids would be better served by being out of the schoolhouse and in the real world with their family and with the community at large." And though everyone around them scoffed and worried, history suggested that these renegades and non-conformists appeared to be right: their kids achieved very highly academically and were ultimately sought after by colleges and universities because they, as a group, proved to be particularly well-prepared for college. Still, one concern nagged at the collective conscious: What about socialization?

As the homeschooling community grew, more and more were asked this question, as though homeschoolers had not thought to consider it. While they tried to explain again and again to no avail, their kids went on learning at alarming rates and developed close, happy friendships with more and more people. As the homeschoolers grew up and moved out into the world as successful, well-adjusted adults, still society demanded of them answers to the same question: What about socialization?

Today millions of families around the world have joined in to experience the countless benefits and unique lifestyle that homeschooling has to offer.

Still, the Big Question remained unanswered—until now.

chapter one

THE SOCIALIZATION QUESTION

"The important thing is to never stop questioning."
—*Albert Einstein*

I will never forget the first day I attended a homeschool play date. It was 12:30 or 1:00 on a sunny Thursday afternoon at a park in Chapel Hill, North Carolina. The park had a play structure and swings, a sandbox larger than my house, a large creek, bridges, and picnic tables. I had a five-year-old son and a one-year-old daughter. The night before, I had phoned a contact person for information about a local homeschool association, and she had invited me to come to this park the next day to meet people and find out more. Having already asked all of the standard questions about homeschooling (including, "Aren't you worried about socialization?"), I went, knowing no one and with few specific expectations except for those inevitable ones that develop through a lifetime of conventional schooling. What I saw that day changed my life, and my children's lives, forever.

The park, which I had seen many times empty except for a few toddlers with parents or nannies here or there, was now positively bustling with children. Some were playing together in the sand; some were picnicking at a table or on a blanket. A few waded in the stream, and several walked around in pairs or groups, talking or exploring the area. One boy lay on a blanket reading. A few parents pushed babies or toddlers in swings; others sat at tables or in portable chairs, talking and laughing with each other and tending to their smaller children when they came asking for help or a snack.

I was astonished to see all of these children happily playing outside in the sunshine in the middle of the day. And more intriguing than that was what I observed when I listened to them interact with each other and with the adults. They were open and articulate, kind and respectful, funny, and enjoyable to be around.

This was definitely news to me.

As a person who was conventionally schooled my entire life—from age two to twenty-two—I had never pictured that such things would, or even could, be going on in the world during school hours. In fact, I thought that school was the place where social life *was*—where friends were found, where life was centered—in short, where it was *at*. The truth is school is indeed where *my* friends were found, because that's where I was most of my waking hours. But, unbeknownst to me, it was not the only place where potential friends existed. Little did I know how much I had to learn.

At one time or another, most of us have asked, been asked, or at least thought the Big Question about homeschooling: "What about socialization?" We have thought it when first hearing of homeschooling. We have asked it out of concern for children we know who are homeschooled. And we have pondered it when tentatively considering alternatives or when frustrated with the quality or cost of our own children's education. In fact, socialization is by far the most frequently expressed concern about homeschooling. (Any homeschooler can tell you this.) The question of socialization falls upon the ears of homeschoolers so often (and is asked in such a doubting tone) that it is often dubbed the "S" word in homeschooling circles.

As a homeschooling parent myself, I find this concern expressed to me so often that it has become a permanent fixture in my life. Wherever I go—the park, the store, businesses, friends' or relatives' houses—I hear it in various forms: "Oh, I've thought about homeschooling, but I don't want my kids to be *isolated*," or "I couldn't handle being *stuck at home*." "My daughter's very social; I can't meet her needs myself," or "I want my kids to be exposed to the *diversity* that you find at school." "Don't you want your kids to learn to deal with others?" "Aren't homeschooled kids alone with their parents all day, isolated from other children, sheltered from all outside influences, starved for peer contact?" "And don't homeschoolers miss out on the rites of passage that come with school, like riding the bus, passing notes in class, dealing with bullies, and going to school dances and football games?"

But that day at the park I caught my first glimpse of a truth that would rock my world—a secret reality that would ultimately change my life and the lives of countless homeschoolers across the globe: that for many families, socialization is actually an *advantage* of homeschooling.

Of course this statement will not go unrefuted, and with good reason. It is an extremely common perception in this culture that homeschoolers are deprived of socialization by not going to school. In fact, many people believe that homeschoolers have virtually no social

3

contact at all. At one time I myself pictured homeschoolers as lonely misfits, incapable of simple conversation and pathetically starving for any kind of interaction with the outside world. In fact, socialization is widely imagined to be a "fatal flaw" of homeschooling.

Paradoxically, though, current research suggests that homeschoolers are actually *better* socialized than their conventionally schooled peers. Though this may at first sound ridiculous or even impossible, in various studies homeschoolers have been found to have higher self-concepts, significantly fewer "problem behaviors," and equal levels of self-esteem compared with their conventionally schooled peers. They also have been described in some studies as being more mature and better socialized (Taylor 1986; Shyers 1992; Smedley 1992; Ray 1999). These findings support the idea that socialization is actually an *advantage* of homeschooling.

But how can this be so?

A clue lies in the lack of collective understanding we, as a culture, share on two major questions: "What is homeschooling?" and "What is socialization?" In today's society there is a general misunderstanding of what homeschooling is, a lack of clarity on what good socialization is, and even a general lack of agreement on what childhood is. It is impossible to address the question of homeschool socialization without first answering these questions.

Perhaps you are thinking, "I already know what homeschooling is. It is the education of a child at home by the parent. I know what socialization is. And I certainly know what childhood is." But, as we will see, the answers to these questions are not as simple or obvious as they may seem. By, "What is homeschooling?" I mean, "What do homeschoolers *really do* when their conventionally schooled counterparts are in the classroom? What kind of lives do they lead?" To know this we must go beyond stereotypical images of homeschooling. We must peer directly into the lives of real homeschoolers.

What the public doesn't know is that homeschooling offers children many social benefits above and beyond what is offered by the institution of school. We don't realize this because most of us do not have the opportunity to see into the lives of real homeschoolers and learn what they do with their time. We imagine that their lives are characterized by an *absence*, an emptiness, which for other children is filled with school. We think of school as a given, and, ironically, have come to view many of the most beneficial social aspects of homeschooling as drawbacks or flaws simply because they are different from a typical school social life. This is the result of a commonly held belief that school is the "gold standard" for socialization, an assumption we will look at in depth in Chapter 3.

I will not suggest in this book that homeschooled kids are exactly the same as traditionally schooled kids. On the whole, they do seem to experience childhood differently and have a different perspective than they would if they went to school, and this difference is not a deficiency. Nor is it my intention to suggest that either homeschooled or traditionally schooled children are "better" or that homeschooling or "schooling" parents are better. Both traditionally schooled and homeschooled kids sometimes have tantrums and moments of brilliance, make mistakes and wise choices, have bad days and good days, and have strengths and weaknesses. Some parents believe that homeschooling is the best environment for their families and have chosen to homeschool for this reason. Each homeschooling parent and homeschooled child has a unique social experience, and it is experiences such as these that I seek to share in this book.

Real people's experiences will show that just as homeschooling works for academics, getting into college, extracurricular activities, and the arts, so, too, can it work for socialization. And soon we will begin to see why many kids and parents love homeschooling *because of*, not despite, socialization.

In fact, on a certain level, homeschooling is all about socialization. Whatever the teaching methods used in school or homeschool, it is ultimately the social environment itself that distinguishes homeschooling from conventional school. This social environment includes the nature and quantity of peer interaction; parental proximity; solitude; relationships with adults, siblings, older children, younger children, and the larger community; the ways in which the children are disciplined and by whom; and even the student-teacher ratio and the overall environment where the children spend their time.

The homeschool social life is indeed different from the school social life in many ways, and it is these very differences (which often cause concern among the public) that make socialization an advantage of homeschooling in the eyes of those experienced with it. And it is these very differences that are leading so many informed families to choose homeschooling for their own children.

In this book we will explore each of the differences one by one. Through the experiences of many real-life homeschoolers, each chapter will shed light on another important aspect of homeschool socialization.

Here are the major social benefits we will explore:

In Chapter 2 we will address some important questions that provide a backdrop for understanding and discussing homeschool socialization, especially the question, "**What do homeschoolers do?**" We will peek into the lives of real homeschoolers to get a clear picture of what their day-to-day lives are really like.

In Chapter 3 we will address the question of **what good socialization actually is**. We will explore common assumptions about the role of school in socialization and whether good socialization can occur without the school environment.

In Chapter 4 we will explore how homeschooling encourages **strong friendships** and healthy, abundant **peer contact** while lessening the need for and tendency toward unhealthy peer dependence. We will look at how peer contact in combination with parental proximity enables children to learn effective social skills that they might otherwise miss out on. By understanding how homeschoolers develop friendships and socialize with peers, we can relax about homeschoolers' peer contact and instead give our kids what they really need for their healthy social development.

In Chapter 5 we will observe how **proximity to parents** and **strong family relationships** benefit children socially, why time with family is a vastly underestimated benefit to children, and why homeschooled children often develop strong, close sibling relationships that strengthen them socially and serve as a model for future relationships. We will discover how the proximity to parents that homeschoolers enjoy actually encourages independence and healthy social behavior and learning. By observing and listening to the real lives, stories, and perspectives of homeschoolers, we will see how living in the security of family-centered rather than school-centered lives actually fortifies homeschoolers to face life's challenges.

In Chapter 6 we will see that homeschooled children benefit from physical, emotional, and social **safety**, such as from bullies and school-related violence, while having enhanced opportunities to develop skills for dealing with future adversity.

In Chapter 7 we will observe how each homeschooled child has abundant **time and freedom to "be a kid"** before having to deal with the pressures of adult life and how this readies children to grow up into healthy adults.

Chapter 8 will address the question of **being "cool"** and reveal that homeschoolers tend not to be controlled by arbitrary, external ideas and dictates of what is "cool." Instead, they create their own definitions of cool that are *more relevant to and in line with the real world.*

Chapter 9 will provide insights into how homeschooling affords children special opportunities for **healthy relationships with adults other than their parents,** including mentoring relationships, friendships, additional role models, and opportunities to get to know grandparents and other adult relatives. This enriches their lives both socially and educationally.

In Chapter 10 we will explore how homeschooling can expose children to true **diversity** and interactions with diverse people in a real-life, meaningful way rather than in the divisive, separatist way found in many schools.

Chapter 11 will reveal why and how homeschoolers become exceptionally well-prepared for **life in the "Real World."** We will address the myth that homeschoolers are sheltered from the "Real World" and discover that the life homeschoolers lead is actually more relevant preparation for "real life" than life in a schoolroom.

Chapter 12 will explore how homeschooled children develop positive senses of **citizenship** and **pluralism** by living, working, and playing in the real world rather than in a classroom.

Chapter 13 will draw on the experiences of adolescent homeschoolers to reveal how homeschooled

teens develop a strong, healthy **sense of self, identity, and independence;** reasons they may or may not choose to go to conventional school at this point; and how they adjust in either circumstance.

In Chapter 14 we will hear from **parents** and learn why they, too, seem to benefit socially from homeschooling and are free to enjoy a rich **social life** while homeschooling responsibly and successfully.

Finally, in Chapter 15, we will see abundant evidence that homeschoolers as a group enjoy remarkable academic success, and we will finally discover the surprising link between the unique **social life** homeschoolers enjoy and this notable **success**.

The question of socialization is one raised time and time again by new homeschoolers, potential homeschoolers, friends, relatives, onlookers, educators, and policymakers alike. And this is quite understandably so, for if homeschooling indeed meant being isolated, stuck at home, and limited in the kinds of people one was exposed to, it would certainly be cause for concern. Parents have a responsibility to consider this important question when choosing how their children will be raised and educated and might be well-advised to pass up the many academic and other benefits of homeschooling if their children were likely to suffer socially as a result.

In fact, socialization may well be the single most important aspect of education today. With high and rising rates of divorce, drug abuse, youth violence, alcoholism, teen promiscuity, and so forth, we cannot afford to let this issue go unexamined. As parents we cannot afford to leave unasked the question of how best to raise our children so they will grow into healthy, happy, and functional adults. We must explore the possibilities, keeping in mind that the current system may or may not be the ideal vehicle for the socialization (and education) of every child. We should also support each other in making the choices that we believe are right for our own individual children. For some families, school may indeed be the best environment; for others it may not. To cling to the idea that what we, as a culture, are doing *now* is the right and best way for *all children* simply because it is what we are used to is to shut our eyes and minds to other possibilities— possibilities that may afford greater happiness, success, peace, and safety to our own children.

At a time when people feel more disconnected than ever before, we cannot afford to overlook or allow ourselves to be blinded to an option that offers great benefits, including a rich, fulfilling, and healthy social life, that our children may well need for the future.

Homeschooling offers great social benefits to kids and parents. And when we understand them, our children are the ones who will win.

chapter two

WHAT DO HOMESCHOOLERS DO?

I hear and I forget.
I see and I remember.
I do and I understand.
—*Chinese proverb*

It seems intrinsically obvious that homeschoolers must be socially deprived. After all, while others are in school, they are not. While schoolchildren ride the school bus, homeschoolers, in general, do not. While the conventionally schooled spend their days with large groups of peers, homeschoolers, it may seem, do not.

But research shows that homeschoolers are not socially deprived. Personal contact with any representative sample of homeschoolers will confirm this. And many experienced homeschoolers consider socialization one of the greatest advantages of homeschooling. Why the discrepancy? One reason is that homeschooling is not what people generally imagine it to be. It is not, as many imagine, essentially school transplanted into the home without the other kids. So just what is it instead? In this chapter we will dispense with common stereotypes and instead peer into

11

the lives of some real homeschoolers to see what they really do with their time.

One definition of homeschooling is that it is simply the education or teaching of a child or children at home, usually by the parent or guardian. To some extent this is true, but for understanding what the life of a homeschooler is really like, this definition is wholly inadequate because in truth, homeschooling is much more than that. It doesn't necessarily take place at home and often has little to do with school. It goes by many names that reflect a variety of approaches and philosophies—homeschooling, unschooling, home-based education, worldschooling, lifeschooling, life learning. I have even heard it jokingly termed "car-schooling"!

The reality is that homeschooling is more than just a home-grown imitation of school, more than an educational method or choice. It is a total child-rearing choice, sometimes a philosophical or religious one, and for many it is nothing short of a way of life.

A Note About "Experts"

You have no doubt seen articles and editorials in the general media that rely on the opinions of school experts, primarily in the form of principals, teachers, and school board personnel, to comment on the pros and cons of homeschooling. This is unfair to both the experts and the public they are speaking to because these individuals are being called upon to comment on something they have little or no knowledge of. Unaware that homeschooling is not "school at home" but something different entirely, these experts invariably explain that homeschoolers miss out on important social experiences. Their concern is genuine, yet their experience lies in the area of school, not homeschool, and they are not able to speak accurately about homeschooling, especially in its social aspects. Still, they are heralded as the authorities on homeschooling and are rarely expected to support their opinions with factual evidence. The National Education Association (NEA), for example, expresses worry about the "fact" that "along with avoiding school violence and unsavory peer influences, home-schooled students often miss out on positive socialization, too," according to a 2003 article in the *Christian Science Monitor.* "No matter what their grades, the criticism goes," says Patrik Jonsson, author of the article, "they're missing a crucial part of the American curriculum: fraternization with peers" (Jonsson 2003).

Everyone wants what is best for the children, and we as a citizenry accept the opinions and recommendations of these "fish-out-of-water" authorities because we do not know what homeschooling really entails. Most people mistakenly believe that homeschooled kids do not spend time with peers, something that is simply not the case. This book will replace these well-meaning "expert" views with the true experiences of the real experts on homeschooling—the people who are doing it day-in and day-out year after year.

In the coming chapters, we will discover that the concerns common in our culture about homeschool socialization are based largely on these erroneous assumptions of what homeschooling actually is. These assumptions persist because most citizens, however concerned, simply don't have access to the facts. Homeschoolers are not easily visible to the rest of the public because most people are either at work or at school all day, making it difficult to obtain an accurate picture of what homeschooling entails at all, much less develop an in-depth understanding of the motivations, methods, consequences, and day-to-day reality of such a misunderstood and sometimes mysterious topic.

What Homeschooling Is Not

The popular image of homeschoolers studying at a desk or the kitchen table all day long, their mothers instructing them in various subjects according to careful lesson plans, isolated from the social world, is misleading. Though some homeschoolers do choose to take a school-like approach or borrow some elements (such as textbooks, chalkboards, tests, recess, and so on) from school, this approach is far less prevalent than popularly assumed. A 1999 study, for example, found that homeschoolers, who as a group are now well-recognized for their academic success, tend not to use pre-packaged curriculum programs and don't tend to spend a lot of money on educational materials (Rudner 1999). Homeschooling expert Patricia Lines agrees: "A media stereotype would have homeschooling children start the day with a prayer and a salute to the flag and then gather around the kitchen table for structured lessons. This is not only atypical, it fails to present the full range of practices" (Lines 2000).

Homeschooling does not mean or require that the children's education takes place in a particular place or within certain designated hours of the day ("school hours"), though some do prefer this type of structure. Homeschooling cannot really be pinned down to a specific description because the very nature of homeschooling is that it is different for every family, and this is part of what makes it work so well. The best we can do is to listen to a variety of real homeschoolers and learn from their experiences.

Some Sample Homeschoolers

While much of the public is in schoolhouses and office buildings each day, there is a whole homeschool community life going on in the outside world. Homeschoolers are at each other's houses playing; gathering in parks; meeting for classes in churches, homes, and public buildings; going on outings and field trips together to museums, zoos, other cities and towns, planetariums, bakeries, concerts, shows, plays, and workshops; sitting on riverbanks having talks with close friends; playing on soccer teams; training on swim teams; rehearsing plays; having parties; painting murals in the community; volunteering; and much more. They learn both in and out of the home—at all hours of the day—at libraries, grandparents' houses, nursing homes, theaters, the beach, Scout meetings, ball games, town meetings, colleges, parks and recreation departments, churches, synagogues, and schools, sometimes alone and often in groups. They are out visiting farms, historical sites, ice skating rinks, and the many other places homeschoolers spend their time.

Of course, many also do formal schoolwork, chores, and so forth, and these activities take only a fraction of the day due to the low student-teacher ratio and the lack of busywork, administrative paperwork, attendance-taking, group discipline, transition time between subjects, and so on. Homeschoolers, like schoolchildren, are eager to get such work done each day so they can go out and play; when work is completed, the rest of the day and evening often remains for other (social) activities.

Lucinda, a twelve-year-old homeschooler from Durham, North Carolina, describes her perception of what the homeschooling life is like for her:

> Mainly it involves practicing the piano and occasionally doing a little bit of math. And seeing friends and stuff. I do mother-helping one day a week, and I also take classes—writing and science class.

15

Since my mom only has to teach two people, instead of twenty people, it's a lot easier because she doesn't have to wait for everybody to finish something or turn in something ... then we either go to the park or whatever.—*Lucinda, homeschooled twelve-year-old, Durham, NC*

Lori, a homeschooling mother of three from Las Vegas, Nevada, describes what her family's homeschooling days are like (the names of the children have been changed to protect their privacy):

Most days (Monday through Saturday) begin with "homework." My children—Brian, Kira, and Jack—are VERY early risers, and if the homework is done before I get up they can then play an educational computer game. ... Then because they both take dance they have a morning stretch routine to complete, followed by piano practice (Brian) and violin (Kira).

My children have a TON of activities, which is why we school six days a week. Monday Kira has dance team, Tuesday and Thursday Jack has preschool, Tuesday Brian and Kira have instrument lessons, Wednesday is choir and sometimes 4H (this is also the day our support group schedules activities), Thursday Brian and Kira have dance and Brian has Boy Scouts, Friday is PE "baby school" when Jack's friend comes over for co-op and Kira has Brownies, Saturday Jack and Kira have gymnastics and Brian has chess, and, of course, church on Sunday. WHEW! Looks awful when you actually write it out—of course, this is BEFORE you add in field trips and occasional or special activities. I usually only get in about two to three hours of instruction per day with all three combined. Because my children are young, we include lots of "fun" stuff: Play Doh, crafts, finger-painting, building with blocks, and reading great children's literature. We also play lots of educational games.

The wonder of it all is that because homeschooling is so efficient, and my children are well-disciplined and eager learners, we can do all the activities, a fairly rigorous academic schedule, and STILL have time for them to ride bikes, play in the backyard, go to friends' houses, play dress up, read to each other, and just plain have fun.

Basically we started this journey for political, social, and educational issues (we were cocky enough to think we could just do it better), and in the last four years it's evolved into a way of life we'd never trade that has given us amazing flexibility to let the children be involved in a variety of activities, spend more time with their father whose non-traditional work schedule we can work around more easily, and learn at their own pace and in their own way. I can't imagine how anyone could hope to meet the needs of thirty-plus different kids who have nothing in common but age, but I admire those who try!—*Lori, homeschooling mother of three, Las Vegas, NV*

Traditional and Less-Traditional Approaches

Homeschooling truly is a million things to a million different people. Some would call it an educational alternative or method, some would call it a philosophy, others might call it a total child-rearing method, and still others might just call it a location. For many, it includes all of these things and more. Always it includes the "academic" education of the children (in some form) and also their social, spiritual, and physical education, though these areas are not necessarily fragmented into "subjects." Even the individual learning environments and methods the parents create or employ are important elements of the homeschool experience.

Homeschoolers follow a variety of approaches. For many, academic work (as such) fits unobtrusively into the day like chores. ("You need to finish your math and make your bed before you go over to Kim's house.") For others, who don't see a need for traditional study methods at all but rather view every part of life as a learning experience, the "academic" aspects are hardly more than incidental, occurring automatically as a natural part of the growing process. "Education is just the whole day, a way of life," says Carol Cosaert, mother of Mindy Cosaert, eleven-year-old finalist in the 2003 Scripps Howard National Spelling Bee, quoted in abcNEWS.com. "It's not just a few hours in the day" (Reynolds 2003).

A family who follows a "traditional" ("school-at-home") approach—the closest to the common image of homeschooling—may devote certain hours of the day to teaching with the aid of a full, published curriculum and may employ such traditional school elements as recess, homework, a chalkboard, desks, standard subject divisions, grades, tests, and the like. Some are enrolled in school part time (Lines 2001; Bielick, et al 2001). Another family may prefer to employ a slightly less traditional approach, such as "unit study," a method in which a topic of interest is selected and studied for a period of time from all perspectives—mathematical, historical, scientific, literary, and so on—before moving on to a new topic or unit. Another family may use other self-designed curricula or methods. Still another family may prefer an "eclectic" approach, taking advantage of whatever methods and materials are best suited to the family's needs at a given time. And another family may follow an unschooling (sometimes called "child-led" or "natural learning") philosophy, allowing the children to direct their own learning according to their interests, personal developmental patterns, and natural curiosity. (These parents generally act as a resource to the children, supporting them as they grow and develop in their own directions, making options and resources available.) Many homeschoolers consider learning an automatic and spontaneous result of day-to-day living, not an isolated, structured activity.

Strange though they may sound, all of these methods are effective and valid. In fact, homeschoolers using each of these methods have won national contests, such as the national spelling bee (Reynolds 2003), and have been accepted to prestigious universities, including Ivy League schools (Foster 2000; Colfax 1988; www.learninfreedom.org).

Still, the vast majority of homeschoolers probably defy categorization. Many who use formal curricula will describe themselves as leaning toward unschooling, or having, philosophically, an "unschoolish" bent. Many self-proclaimed unschoolers dabble in formal curriculum pieces, such as math, handwriting, and others.

Parthy, a homeschooling mother of two from Minnesota, says:

> I have two children, fourteen and ten, who have been homeschooled all their lives. We tend toward the unschooling side of things, though both kids ask me to order them a little curriculum. We usually use pieces of the Oak Meadow curriculum (math for my younger daughter, Latin and history for my older), which they basically work on when and where they want to. All I insist upon is that they finish the curriculum they asked me to order before I order more!—*Parthy, homeschooling mother of two, Minnesota*

A large number of homeschooling parents will describe their approach as eclectic, not subscribing to any specific approach but rather just using whatever works at a given time. Many also evolve over the years, starting out with one method or approach, and gradually discover that their children thrive best with more or less structure and adjust accordingly. The nature of homeschooling is that there is flexibility to do whatever suits the family's needs.

Jane, a homeschooling mother of two—ages eleven and thirteen—from Minnesota, explains her family's approach:

> We've just completed two years of homeschooling. We defy categorization. We use Saxon math. I teach history, writing, grammar, critical thinking, and geography through literature. To complement all this, we participate in a secular homeschool co-op. Simply, we homeschool for academic and SOCIAL reasons.
>
> Academically, my kids move at the speed dictated by their skills and interests, not by the slowest group of students in a classroom. We, as a family, can pursue special interests that would never find their way into a formal "classroom." If we want to study until midnight because we're excited, we can. To study statistics we can play Black Jack, even Poker. Our "school day" is significantly shorter than the public or private school day. We have time to be with one another without the dictates of homework and extracurricular requirements of most schools.
>
> Succinctly, we have a life—a rich life that is not defined only by government school, its homework, and social constructs.—*Jane, homeschooling mother of two, Minnesota*

Social activities can fall into a similar range of options. Whereas one family may engage in structured academics in the morning followed by social playtime with friends in the afternoon, another family may prefer to gather with other homeschoolers to explore topics of interest in a social manner or setting. Families who engage in little or no formal "sit-down" academics may have lots of time to simply play and discover the world with friends or in the comfort of the family, as they see fit.

And homeschool life often occurs in groups. Jane, the Minnesota mother from above, describes a cooperative homeschool group her family belongs to:

Called Wind and Water Homeschool Co-op, it neatly addresses bothacademic and social requirements. Academically, parents teach as they have the skill, training, or desire, or we hire outside instruction.Ours has been a commitment to teaching excellence, with price andaffordability a secondary factor. This is a town with many institutions of higher learning, and we take advantage of that community to recruit our young, enthusiastic outside instructors. Strong in science, language arts, novel studies, history, art, and computer skills, our co-op leaves math (except for certain contextual math) to the individual families.—*Jane, homeschooling mother of two, Minnesota*

To put it another way, homeschoolers often engage in family-based, rather than school-based, living and learning and full-time access to the real world and community. Education is not necessarily separated from social life. They are part and parcel, sometimes even one and the same.

Missy, a mother of two from North Carolina, describes how family-based education works in her household:

Well, it's living life. Whether we get up and make breakfast together, whether we're working in the kitchen doing stuff, we just spend time together. And while we're spending that time together, things come up for science experiments and math and reading, and it's not like there's a structure to "okay, now we're going to do schooling" or "okay, now we're not going to do schooling." It just blends in; it's just a continual flow.

We live in a neighborhood, so we get a lot of kids around our house. In the summer, it's all day. When school's in, it's when school's out [for the day] and the other kids have gotten done with their homework they'll come over. Or it's through one of the two homeschooling groups we belong to. ... [My son] also belongs to a Tai Kwon Do gym. He has lots of friends there, so we pretty much spend time there. Kids will come home or he'll go over there, so it's interaction as the days meld.—*Missy, homeschooling mother of two, Cary, NC*

Following are some things real homeschoolers interviewed for this book do with their days:

- Group play dates
- Private play dates with a friend
- Read freely
- Cook
- Clean up creeks and natural areas
- Travel
- Self-directed book work
- Historical reenactment
- Take classes with other homeschoolers
- Attend classes in the community
- Attend church, synagogue, and so forth
- Play a musical instrument or take music lessons
- Write stories and poems
- Swim on a swim team
- Horseback riding or lessons
- Help on a farm
- Drama classes
- Debate clubs

- Knitting groups
- Birthday parties
- Ice skating
- Make video movies together
- Write, direct, and act in plays
- History clubs
- Science clubs
- Hebrew school or Sunday school
- Hold craft shows and sales
- Hold public readings of original stories or poetry
- Babysit
- Be babysat
- Form singing groups; rehearse and perform concerts
- Build tree houses
- Watch people fix cars
- Spend the afternoon reading at the library
- Go to the ballet or other shows
- Martial arts classes
- Dance classes or dance company
- Attend social dances in the community
- Attend homeschool dances
- Use the computer or surf the Internet
- Write songs
- Play guitars around campfires
- Camp in groups
- 4-H club
- Scouts
- Make sand castles on the beach
- Sleepovers
- Share skills with younger kids
- Improv drama class or mime class
- Go to the movies
- Attend Renaissance Faires
- Volunteer at a Street Festival booth
- Work on a political campaign

- Stop and talk to homeless people
- Stop and talk to store employees and owners
- Stop and talk to parents
- Spend the afternoon at a favorite part of the science museum
- Art museum
- History museum
- Play with neighbors
- Swim with friends at neighborhood pool
- Build stuff with Mom or Dad
- Form quilting group and make a quilt for a women's shelter
- Paint
- Draw
- Form a Lego group and enter tournaments
- Travel with family or friends
- Help with Mom's day camp
- Hold own day camp, if old enough
- Perform in local puppet or theater productions
- Attend Kwanzaa festival
- Relax in yard and watch clouds
- Open a detective agency
- Get up at 4 AM to watch meteor shower
- Watch video and eat popcorn with family
- Have a relaxed lunch with Mom
- Chat
- Visit grandparents
- Have long talks with relatives
- Take care of pets
- Play baseball
- Take walks
- Organize or participate in a science fair
- Publish a literary magazine
- Submit articles or stories to a magazine
- Holiday parties
- Write letters to congressmen

- Read the newspaper
- Bake cookies
- Cook dinner
- Make pottery
- Buy food at farmer's market and get to know vendors
- Set up a lemonade stand
- Make forts with siblings
- Explore the woods with friends
- Climb trees
- Take naps
- Get up early
- Sleep late
- Design clothes
- Conduct science experiments
- Write letters to pen pals or key pals
- Read to younger brother or sister
- Play on local soccer teams
- Play in the river
- Trick-or-treat
- Attend political demonstrations, rallies, and so on
- Ask questions
- Archery classes

Busy with these types of real-life activities, homeschoolers are not "stuck at home," but are free to come and go, in and out of the home, as they see fit. I have heard homeschoolers refer to themselves as "never-at-home-schoolers," and this is why. They have ample time to spend alone, with family, with other homeschoolers, and with the community at large.

Homeschooling Is
Family-Based Living

But perhaps the most important unifying factor among all homeschoolers, and the one that truly makes the homeschooling lifestyle what it is, is that the homeschooling family shares their days. The members of the family share one unified life rather than leading separate lives (for example, lives at school, at work, and so on) that intersect only in the evening and on weekends. This is cited as a key feature of homeschooling even by single-parent families and families in which the parents work outside the home. Through all the talking and listening I have done with hundreds of diverse homeschoolers across the country, one common theme emerged as the most important advantage to homeschoolers: family unity. As we will see in Chapter 5, this element of homeschooling is of the utmost importance to homeschoolers, who consider it the cornerstone of (and the greatest boon to) their children's social development. Whatever approach a homeschooling family follows, they do it in a family context, a setting that we all continue to live in, need, and experience our entire lives, rather than in a school setting, which is an artificial environment that exists only during childhood and is not duplicated later in life unless one becomes a teacher.

Within the homeschooling lifestyle, families are free to spend frequent, extended periods of time with other families or groups of families, socializing with the other kids and adults while still remaining in the presence of their own families. Since the children move in the same circles as their parents, it is easy for them to spend time with their friends while the adults spend time with theirs. At the same time the family remains physically unified and the parents remain present for and available to the children, who can be supervised on an age-appropriate basis. This type of social gathering is, for many, an integral part of the homeschooling experience. (This is explained in great detail in Chapter 5, with many examples from real homeschoolers.) Certainly homeschool kids and adults also have some of their own separate friends from other circles, too, but it seems they are far less likely to feel disenfranchised from one another.

Linda, a homeschooling mother of four from Niagara Falls, New York, talks about how many consider family unity the biggest benefit of homeschooling:

> I was working on a master's degree in education when my children were three years old and newborn. In fact, I took my six-week-old son to [the university] with me to complete my last class. For this class we had to choose from a list of topics to do a research paper. I chose homeschooling. I never even heard of homeschooling until I called a [breastfeeding counselor] for help after my first was born and she said she was homeschooling her children. "Is that legal?" was my thought. By the time I completed my research paper, I was so impressed with homeschooling that I thought it might be something for my family. When I finished my research paper, I summarized that people homeschool for a variety of reasons, but all claim "family unity" to be the biggest benefit.—Linda, homeschooling mother of four, Niagara Falls, NY

The homeschool family functions largely as a unit at home as well, having abundant time to get to know each other well and learn skills for living together. That learning is as much a part of homeschooling as learning math or reading is. At the same time, the very small

27

ratio and the unique parent-child relationship homeschooling facilitates (which we will discuss further in Chapter 5) allows parents a great deal of room to understand, respect, and nourish their children's individuality.

Why People Choose Homeschooling

There is a wide range of reasons why people choose homeschooling. Most common among them are family unity, academic success, more flexible methods and other freedoms, and socialization. Surprisingly enough, those who homeschool for primarily religious reasons are actually in the minority among homeschoolers (Lines 2000; Bauman 2001).

According to the U.S. Census Bureau (2001), in 1996 and 1999 surveys, homeschooling parents cited the following reasons (from a list of choices) for choosing homeschooling: Half of all homeschoolers surveyed said they were doing so because they felt it was better educationally. Thirty-three percent cited religion as one reason, and nine percent cited morality. Practical considerations and cost were not major factors, although these benefits do exist for many homeschoolers (Bauman 2001). ("Socialization" and "family unity" were not listed as options for parents to choose on this survey.)

Some homeschoolers also cite frustrations with or shortcomings of schools as a factor. According to the Census Bureau, 30 percent felt that "regular" school had a "poor learning environment," 14 percent disapproved of subject matter taught in schools, and 11 percent cited a lack of challenging material at school (Bauman 2001).

The National Home Education Research Institute also names other key reasons families choose homeschooling, including values education; closeness in family relationships; alternative educational approaches; "controlled and positive social interactions;" and the physical, psychological, social, sexual, and drug-related safety of the children (NHERI, "Fact Sheet IIe" 2000). Other homeschoolers name further advantages: ability to control the child's *primary* environment (this does not mean they keep them in that environment all the time, but rather that they can influence the nature of the normal environment to fortify the child for when he ventures out of that environment), schedule (and other types of) flexibility, less wasted time, the absence of stress and fear elements in the learning (and social) process, more individual attention, and control over the type of discipline used on the children (Stewart 1990).

Social education

For most homeschooling parents, the non-academic education (such as social, spiritual, ethical, and values) is as important a part of homeschooling as is the academic. (Many homeschoolers consider it *more* important.) Two women share their point of view on the matter:

I am not currently a homeschooling mom, but I hope to be. I am not so interested in doing it for religious reasons as for educational and philosophical reasons—one of those being positive socialization with people of all ages, not just socialization with their peer groups. I am also interested in raising independent thinkers who aren't concerned about going along with the crowd and with the popular, consumer society just in order to fit in.—*Amy, Clayton, NY*

29

> Why I decided to homeschool was that [my daughter] was unhappy at school because of the way she was being treated by her classmates, and she was also unhappy because of the way she was interacting with the teachers and material.—*Christine, homeschooling mother of one, Durham, NC*

According to the National Home Education Research Institute, researcher Dr. Johnson, after studying homeschooling families, concluded that homeschooling parents are highly attentive to addressing their children's socialization needs (NHERI 2003). Homeschool parents have plenty of time to devote to teaching and encouraging positive social skills. The question of what these positive social skills might be, and whether the children can, and indeed, do learn them through homeschooling, is the subject of the remainder of this book.

Who Homeschools?

Another misunderstood aspect of homeschooling that leads to socialization concerns is the question of *who* homeschoolers are. The common idea that homeschoolers are a very specific, homogeneous segment of the population is a simple misconception. Just as there are a variety of methods and philosophies, there are lots of different types of families as well. There are homeschooling families with twelve kids and families with one. There are very rich families, very poor families, and everything in between. There are urban, suburban, and rural families and families from every part of the country and world. There are traditional and non-traditional families, religious and non-religious families, Christian, Jewish, Muslim, atheist, agnostic, and none of the above. There are families with adopted children and families made up of wonderful mixtures of backgrounds, nationalities, and races. There are homeschooling parents and kids of every race, political affiliation, sexual orientation, marital status, and so on (Cordes 2000; NHEN, "Homeschool Soup;" Bauman 2001).

According to Patricia M. Lines, former Department of Education homeschool researcher, homeschoolers do seem to be *more likely* than the average American family to be "religious, conservative, white, better educated, and part of a two-parent family" (Lines 2001). At the same time, as Lines also points out, homeschooling families hail from "all major ethnic, cultural, and religious backgrounds and all income levels" (Lines 2001). And the numbers of families who do not fit the "profile," including minority families, single-parent families, non-religious, lower- or higher-income, non-conservative, and so forth families, are very rapidly growing. There is no paucity of diversity in the homeschooling community today. The issue of diversity among homeschoolers will be discussed in greater detail in Chapter 9.

So What is Homeschooling?

Ultimately, homeschooling really comes down to two things. The factors that make homeschooling what it is are family-centered living and real-world, community-based learning. As we will see in the following chapters, it is these factors that create the unique (social) setting in which homeschoolers live, learn, and grow. And it is through understanding this unique social setting that we can begin to answer the important and so-often asked question of homeschool socialization, and we can finally explore the many social benefits of homeschooling.

But first we must address one more important question: Just what is socialization? This may sound like a simple question, but, as we will see in the next chapter, cultural bias may have blocked our understanding of this important issue. And answering it is the key to understanding the socialization of homeschoolers and school children alike.

chapter three

WHAT IS GOOD SOCIALIZATION, ANYWAY?

"It is no measure of health to be well adjusted to a profoundly sick society."—Krishnamurti

Socialization is important. There is no doubt about that. No one wants their child to be a "misfit;" no one wants their child to be lonely, unhappy, or unprepared for future relationships. This is no doubt why the question of children's socialization is an issue for *all* parents and is a particularly common focus when people think or inquire about homeschooling. Parents, quite rightly, want their children to grow up in a healthy and proper social environment. Concerned citizens want all children to have this opportunity as well.

But unless we know exactly what healthy socialization is, we cannot determine what kind of environment encourages it or even whether children—homeschooled, traditionally schooled, or otherwise—are properly or improperly socialized. So just what is good socialization?

This may seem like a simple enough question. But

though everyone agrees that socialization is important, there is no commonly understood and accepted definition of "good" socialization. It is not enough to say that good socialization means being "normal." Every individual develops her own idea of what socialization (and even "normal") means and what it should be. There is no standardized test at the end of high school rendering a socialization score, no common objectives for socialization over the course of schooling. There is only happiness and the ability to function well in the world. And even these are very personalized matters.

Indeed, socialization is a very personal concept. We must all choose what kind of socialization we want or feel is appropriate for our children. Is it an ability to "fit in"? To be comfortable being oneself? To get along with others, to stand up for oneself, or both? To blend in or to walk away in the face of peer pressure? Is it preparation to belong to a group? To lead it? The interpretations and perspectives abound. Likewise, as pointed out earlier, the question, "What about socialization?" asked of homeschoolers by a hundred different people can mean a hundred different things. Do homeschoolers have friends? Self-esteem? Do they hold down jobs when they grow up? Are they "cool"? Do their parents smother them? How will they learn to deal with bullies? Learn independence? Sometimes it means one of these things, sometimes several, and sometimes something completely different. One thing is certain: socialization remains an elusive, abstract concept that parents, educators, and citizens alike fear because, in the end, we simply do not know what it is.

To Fit or Train?

According to Webster, to "socialize" is defined as "to fit or train for a social environment." But *what kind of* social environment is not specified. What environment should our children be "fit or trained" for? Society as it is today? Society as it is likely to be when the children grow up? Society as we *want* it to be when they grow up? Our own family or religious or cultural group? Someone else's? A school environment? The "outside" world? Who decides what is an appropriate social environment to fit or train our children for?

When we ask whether a child is being properly socialized, the question is ambiguous—even almost meaningless—until we identify what the desired outcome of socialization is in the perspective of the asker. (We could easily answer the specific question, "Does he have friends?" or "Is she comfortable in groups?" or "Does he have table manners?" but the general question "Is she getting socialized?" is not so simple.) We do not always identify the desired outcome because we unknowingly rely on an unspoken, unnoticed, and unexamined assumption: that school *is* socialization.

The definition also leaves unanswered the question of *how* the fitting or training takes place or should take place and also what "fit" or "trained" looks like in finished form (that is, how one knows if a person has been fit and trained properly). Would they be "cool"? Respectable? Respect*ful*? Blend in with the other kids or rise above the rest of the crowd?

Everyone has a different answer to these questions. But perhaps we can at least agree that one common social environment we all want to "fit or train" our children for is adulthood itself.

One homeschooling mother shares her perspective:

> You do have to function at a level so that you
> can maneuver in our society, and of course there's
> no bad effect of homeschooling on that. You're still
> living your life; you're just not doing it in a

classroom. You'd have to live alone in a box or something like that to not learn how to maneuver around in society.—*Christine, homeschooling mother of one, Durham, NC*

Is Socialization Being "Made Social"?

When visiting the park, I sometimes meet people who are walking their dogs, taking care to give them a chance to be around other animals (and sometimes people), because they are "socializing" them. Used in this way, socialization means getting the animals used to being around people and treating people and other dogs the way their humans want them to. We might imagine that we also have to do this with human children, but we don't. Pets must be trained and socialized because they are outside of their natural social environment. A dog growing up among other dogs in the wild would not need to be consciously "socialized" because it is biologically programmed to interact with the other dogs in the pack the way dogs are supposed to (and they learn it automatically from their parents and other pack members). Indeed, any dog owner will tell you that this is why dogs make such good pets—they are pack animals and naturally social. So, too, are humans naturally social. We are biologically programmed to be social with our own kind—namely, other humans.

And in the most basic way, human beings are inherently social creatures. All over the world, in all known cultures throughout history, people instinctively seek out other people; our natural grouping is the family, and the vast majority of humans are naturally drawn into larger groups, such as tribes, villages, towns, or other communities, due to our innate need for each other's companionship, help, and support. We have feelings built in that reveal and ensure our continued social nature, since this is necessary for us to survive and thrive. We feel lonely and even afraid without others and comfortable and happy when we have positive relationships with others. Like hunger and thirst, these feelings exist because they ensure our survival and continued health. As babies, we cry when left alone and smile when spoken to. From birth on, we are driven to be with other people (starting with our mothers, fathers, and siblings and moving ever outward), to interact with them, to both imitate and differentiate from them, to play, and to learn at an incredible rate the language that we need to communicate with other human beings.

Because of this inherently social nature, human children do not have to be "social-ized" in the sense of being *made social*. They are, quite simply, born social.

Socialization Is Social Learning

However, we do have to learn social skills and concepts, in much the same way we have to learn other skills that come naturally to humans, such as talking, walking, and eating solid foods. From this perspective, social learning is an area of learning like any other. Learning social skills is something no more difficult to learn than any other skill, as long as we have someone (usually an adult or older child) to model these skills for us. Social skills can be learned in a family context just as easily as every other skill can. Just as kids can and do learn successfully in other areas in homeschooling, so can and do they learn social skills and concepts effectively and successfully in homeschooling. Just as homeschooling works well for academic learning, so does it work well for social learning.

37

In fact, the prerequisites for healthy social growth—love, security, compassion, discipline, and so on—are found primarily in the family.

If socialization is indeed just social learning, though, this raises the question of *what* social skills and attitudes the children learn or should learn and who decides. It includes learning *about* the social world as well as living within it, and we can choose how we want our kids to learn about that. Do we want them to learn that people socialize only with people of their own age, intelligence level, or socio-economic group, or do we want them to learn that the world is full of interesting people of all ages and walks of life? Shall we teach them how to interact on a day-to-day basis with people they love or mainly with people they hardly know? And then there remains the question of how best these skills and attitudes can be learned. Homeschoolers believe they can best be learned in a family-centered, community-based context, and we will hear their reasons for that throughout the rest of this book.

Is School the "Gold Standard"?

But there is also a hidden meaning often attributed to socialization: school-based socialization (or what I like to call "schoolization"). Many believe that homeschoolers cannot get properly socialized simply because they do not get *school-based* socialization, the logic being that regardless of other factors, without going to school a child simply cannot be socialized because school is the place where socialization occurs. In the absence of a true standard for socialization, some cultures look to this, the only place they know to look. A culture made up of people who have almost universally been taught, socialized, and raised in schools unquestioningly assumes that school-based socialization *is* socialization, or at least is the right or best kind of socialization.

This is understandable, since most people know no other way to accomplish these things, never having seen them happen any other way. In fact, most think of school as inseparable from socialization because school has become, in people's minds, inseparable from childhood itself. Some people cannot imagine childhood without it because they cannot imagine their own childhoods without it.

In many ways society unconsciously defines good childhood socialization in terms of similarity to the behavior of a typical school-going child. Anyone who acts, thinks, and looks like a "typical" school child (or school-educated person) is considered "normal," and all others are abnormal. The school experience itself has come to be viewed as the definition of a "normal" childhood. In light of this widespread unconscious assumption, it is no surprise that school, despite its many flaws and downsides, is considered by many to be the ideal place to become socialized. After all, if acting like you've gone to school were the goal of social education, then school would indeed be the only place where such a quality could really be acquired.

Although what we all really want for our children is happy childhoods and the chance for them to grow up into happy, functional adults with the skills to have successful relationships, we tend to forget this and instead focus on comparing children's social experience to an unquestioned "norm"—the typical school experience—that may in fact have little to do with this goal. Any difference or "missing" element (for example, riding the bus) is automatically seen as a lack, even without examining whether that element is important or even helpful to the objective of positive social learning. While they may not act and feel "like schoolchildren," homeschooled children, their parents maintain, are acquiring the real skills they need to succeed in life both academically and socially.

In fact, despite the fact that compulsory schooling has existed in the United States for over two hundred years now, the rates of divorce, crime, drug abuse, suicide, and dysfunction of various kinds are as high as or higher than ever. Still, as a culture we persist in believing that school is a necessary and ideal source of socialization for children. Naturally, schools cannot be blamed for these problems, since it is not schools but parents who are responsible for the social and emotional education and growth of children. It is not in schools but in homes that these types of problems originate and develop. Psychologist John Gray, Ph.D., in his book *Children Are From Heaven*, says, "Our children's problems begin in the home and can be solved at home" (Gray 1999). Indeed, the family is responsible for a child's social, behavioral, spiritual, and even academic upbringing, and many studies have shown that parents and home life are by far the strongest influencing factors in all these areas.

If schools were necessary for healthy social development, then nearly the whole of mankind would have been utterly unable to function interpersonally until the advent of compulsory schooling just two hundred years ago. And yet the human race has successfully carried on, co-existed, and grown since its inception, bringing us right up to modern times. Members of the earlier human race were socialized in the real world—that is, in families and communities.

Today there is a widespread illusion that school is a crucial and definitive source of social activity for children. Without school, the thinking goes, children would have no friends, no birthday parties to go to, no fun—in short, no social life.

But despite the common image of school as a smorgasbord of friends and social activity for children, kids, as a general rule, do not want to be there. It is no secret that some kids dislike school.

Fortunately, kids are naturally social. They don't need a singular institution to help them find friends and fun things to do. Friends are everywhere. In the neighborhood, at church, synagogue, or other religious groups, at Scouts, and so on. In fact, once I had glimpsed the lives of people who lived their days unfettered by school schedules and restrictions, I discovered a jarring truth: School actually *interferes* with social life. I realize that will sound ridiculous, as it would have to me at one time, but I assure you, you'll see what I mean. In Chapter 4 we will hear numerous quotes from homeschoolers describing the surprising ways that homeschooling has actually helped them to have more time with friends and a fuller, more fun social life. In Chapter 5 they will explain how family unity encourages and allows kids to experience more time with friends and have a still fuller, healthier social life. Again and again I hear homeschoolers I interview tell me that homeschooling allows them more time with friends than they had in school.

Elizabeth, a homeschooling mother of two from Raleigh, North Carolina, and T.J., a homeschooled nine-year-old from Durham, North Carolina, share their stories:

> We've been homeschooling—it's been two full years now.
>
> I pulled [my daughter] out in January of her fourth-grade year, and she's a sixth-grader now.
>
> I realized that those two hours of homework I was helping her with each day all those years, that was me homeschooling. We sat down and figured out how much work we were doing at

home. ... What life do they have when they spend all their time in class and doing homework? —*Elizabeth, homeschooling mother of two, Raleigh, NC*

[I like] that you don't have to get up really early and go outside, and I like having pets at "school." I have more time now [than when I went to school] to play with friends. We like to walk around, talk, and explore in the woods a lot.

I spend a lot of time hanging out with my brothers, too. I like hanging out with my brothers. You just have more time with your friends.—*T. J., homeschooled nine-year-old, Durham, NC*

At a time when it's common to hear stories on the news about school violence, children shooting each other, bullying, and so on, it simply does not make sense to continue to hold school up as the obvious standard source of great socialization.

But with all the talk in the media about how "hard" homeschool parents have to work to provide their kids with educational resources and social interaction, the public has come to imagine that homeschoolers in general are in a constant uphill battle to imitate traditional schooling in all its various aspects. Luckily, this is not the case.

In a country where parents (and kids) are choosing homeschooling over traditional schooling at a rate of 10-20 percent more per year, many of them citing social reasons, we can no longer continue to consider school the unquestioned standard by which to judge all alternatives. Families are leaving school because they want something *better* for their kids. As we will see, many homeschooling parents cite social problems and safety at school as primary factors in their decisions to homeschool (see Chapter 5). Despite the valiant efforts of perhaps thousands of dedicated and skilled teachers, administrators, and policy-makers, schools—or maybe the institution of school itself—are failing educationally and socially. This is nothing new; parents have long been concerned about the shortcomings of the school system, but they never knew there was an alternative until now. Now that they know, they are flocking out the schoolhouse doors.

The naked truth is that school is the definitive gold standard for only one type of socialization: school-based socialization. But there is another kind of socialization, and this is the one many homeschoolers are after: family- and community-based socialization.

Even John Dewey, probably the most significant and influential educational thinker of the twentieth century, said that school has become artificially removed and separated from society to the extent that it is "the one place in the world where it is most difficult to get experience" (Lines 2000). Homeschoolers, rather than being removed from society in school and trained for *school* life, are instead living their day-to-day lives in the real world.

If the question, "Do homeschoolers get properly socialized?" really meant, "Will they grow up feeling and acting exactly the same as if they had gone to school?" then the answer would certainly be "no."

But if good socialization is defined as learning or acquiring the ability to function well and be happy in society, then that is a whole different question, and in the answer to that question lie many of homeschooling's great benefits.

Family- and Community-Based Socialization

Family- and community-based socialization is the experience of growing up and learning socially in the family and larger community rather than in a classroom or other "removed" environment. It consists of living and interacting in the real world on a day-to-day basis. Whereas schools are in some ways artificial "models" of adult life, cut off from the real community and economy, family- and community-based life exists in the real world (Guterson 1992). It involves having real-life, meaningful interactions and conversations with people of all age groups, appearances, walks of life, socio-economic groups, and so on in all settings, including on the job, at home, in parks, in classes, at parties, and even in nursing homes, hospitals, libraries, on the telephone, and the list goes on.

Family- and community-based socialization is composed of a) low-ratio attention from adults who are usually the parents of the child; b) a large quantity of contact with siblings (if applicable), with guidance from parents; c) one-on-one and group contact with other kids; and d) contact on a friendship-, mentoring-, or authority-figure basis with various other adults.

Homeschooling mother and author Lee Stewart says, "It is my opinion that the purpose of the family situation is to give the family members the opportunity of learning to get along well with a few people so they can, in turn, learn to get along with many in the larger families of their community and the world. In my opinion," she continues, "this is the most important advantage of homeschool" (Stewart 1990).

Common Concerns

Ultimately, when people ask homeschoolers the ubiquitous question, "What about socialization?" they may really be asking any of the following things:

"Is he cool?"

"Does she spend a lot of time with peers?"

"How much is he like a school-going child?"

"Does she have any freedom or spend time away from her parents?"

"Does he like his parents?" (Sometimes liking parents is viewed as a positive trait, sometimes as a negative.) "Like being away from them? Feel comfortable being away from them?"

"Does she have friends? How many? How close?"

"Does he have run-ins with bullies?"

"Does she know her 'place'?" (That is, relative to adults.)

"Will he be prepared to cheerfully enter the workforce at the end of childhood?"

"Will she be exposed to diversity?"

"Will he be a good citizen? Be exposed to the ways of democracy?"

"Will she be able to function in society?"

"Will he get to be a kid?"

And the list goes on.

Some of these questions are relevant to whether the child is being prepared for future social life; some are not. Each component or sub-meaning must be addressed separately because each is really a distinct question. Socialization is not *one* of these things, but all of them and more. And when it comes to the question of whether one is well-socialized or whether a particular educational setting can offer proper socialization, the answer lies largely in how you define the terms.

In the end, each of these questions is an expression

45

of the larger concern that we all share about all of our children. In our own ways, we are each asking, "Is the child happy and learning to become a healthy, functional adult? Will she be *okay*?"

Perhaps most of us can agree that ultimately the goal of childhood socialization is a happy childhood followed by a happy, healthy, functional adult life in which the individual is well-prepared with skills for real-world relationships. That is probably what we all want for our children. How best to achieve this is another question—one that there is much debate over—and that we will explore over the coming chapters.

If we keep in mind that a happy childhood and a happy, functional adulthood are the goal and mark of good socialization, we can finally begin to explore the many social benefits of homeschooling, starting with one of the most commonly raised areas of concern: friends and peer contact.

chapter four

FRIENDS AND
PEER CONTACT

*"Not everything that counts can be counted, and not
everything that can be counted counts."*
—*Albert Einstein*

*"An hour with friends is worth more than ten with
strangers."*—*Chinese fortune cookie*

Without a doubt, the single most common fear
people express about homeschoolers' social
lives is that they will lack peer contact. When they ask
the question, "What about socialization?" many are
really asking, "Will they get to interact with large
numbers of other kids?" In most cases, if the asker had
a chance to view the lives of homeschoolers, this concern
would probably melt away, since homeschooling affords
children plenty of healthy peer contact, as well as the
safety, guidance, and social learning provided by
parental proximity.

Homeschooled Peers

Homeschoolers do have peers, of course. There may have been a time when homeschoolers were more scarce or isolated, but today, with the number of homeschoolers in the US estimated in the millions—and that number growing at a rate of 10 to 20 percent per year (Bauman 2001)—isolation is simply no longer a real threat to homeschoolers who seek peer contact. To begin with, they have plenty of other homeschooled peers to spend time with; in fact, many homeschoolers belong to a homeschool association or group that meets regularly for play, class-sharing, and so on. Some belong to a closer-knit homeschool community that interacts frequently as well. Many parents do not make the decision to homeschool until they find (or know they can find) a group to belong to. Parents who choose to homeschool, like others, tend to start out with concerns about socialization and often demand of other homeschoolers the same answers about socialization that are later demanded of them.

At the same time, parents who do not belong to such a community or group do not necessarily feel that their kids are missing out on socialization, a fact that will be discussed later in this chapter and in other chapters as well.

With or without a group, homeschoolers play and work with homeschooled friends, organizing playgroups, networks, communities, field trips, classes, and clubs. They also go over to each other's houses or play at parks while their school-going counterparts are in the classroom. In a study conducted by Dr. Brian Ray, president of the National Home Education Research Institute, it was found that the average homeschooler participates in at least five major social activities away from home each week, including classes, sports, theater,

Scouts, clubs, and youth groups (Ray 1999). These children have real time with friends to engage in long talks and develop interests together in a pressure-free environment. They often develop deep friendships—without having to covertly pass notes or talk in class at the risk of getting in trouble and without having to grab a minute or two between classes at the risk of being late. As more and more people homeschool, the number of kids available during school hours is rapidly growing. It will not be long before we will walk out our doors and find that homeschoolers are simply everywhere.

Lucinda, a twelve-year-old homeschooler from Durham, North Carolina, comments on her feelings about her social life:

> I like that I have a lot of different friends, like friends that are older than me and younger than me. I think I have as many friends as I would like, and I do get to see them enough. With different friends I do different stuff. Like with [one friend] I usually play "self" games—pretend games—where we pretend to be other characters and make up our lives and stuff. And with other friends I play games a lot, like board games, a creator game, and a card game that we always play. Some of my friends come from my neighborhood, some from moms (kids of my mom's friends), and some from homeschooling. They come to play dates [with the homeschool group]. I meet them, and we become friends. I think I find myself around a lot of different people. A lot of my friends don't like to play sports, or they don't necessarily like the same music as I do, or they don't like the same games or books. ... I think it's a good thing because then you can try some of what they do, and you might learn to like new stuff.
>
> [Some people] say, "You don't have recess?" But it's because [the schooling] doesn't take as long.

I just think that all of those people who think homeschoolers don't see people are just wrong, because it's not true.—*Lucinda, homeschooled twelve-year-old, Durham, NC*

Conventionally Schooled Peers

Of course, homeschoolers don't live in a vacuum; they also have conventionally schooled peers in the neighborhood, at church or synagogue, at Scouts, at youth group, on sports teams, and so forth—the same places and sources that conventionally schooling families rely on for much of their kids' real (or best) socialization. Some also participate in extracurricular activities at public schools, and some even attend school part-time (Lines 2001; Bielick, et al 2001).

"School hours"

It is important to remember that it is only during school hours that homeschoolers are separate from school children. Outside of school hours all children are in the same situation socially, except of course that homeschooled children, by that time of day, often don't have homework to spend time on.

"In any case," says George Abraham Thampy, twelve-year-old winner of the 2000 Scripps Howard National Spelling Bee, "just because I don't go to a big classroom full of other children my age doesn't mean I'm lonely. I have brothers and sisters and other home-schooled friends, not to mention Boy Scout friends, and friends around the neighborhood and church. I have no trouble relating to kids who go to conventional schools" (Thampy 2000).

Socializing in school?

One question homeschoolers have raised is this: "Is peer contact in school, in fact, social?"

Recently on an airplane, I was seated next to an eleven-year-old girl, whom I will call "Diana"—a sixth-grader from Rhode Island. She looked bored, and it was a three-hour flight, so I struck up a conversation with her. After a minute, I thought to offer her one of the children's books I had in my bag.

"Do you like books?" I asked her.

"Not really," she said.

Surprised, I decided to just make friendly chit-chat instead. "What do you like to do?" I asked.

She replied, "Nothing."

After a pause, I remembered I also had paper and pencils, so I tried, "Do you like to draw?"

"No, not really," she said.

There was a period of quiet. Then, trying to make further conversation, I asked, "Do you like school?"

"No," said Diana.

"Why not?" I asked.

"It's boring," she said. "You learn things you could learn from your parents."

I persisted. "But you get to hang out with the other kids, right?"

Diana shrugged. "At lunch."

"You don't have other time to hang out with them?" I asked.

With another shrug, she replied, "Not really. We're too busy on our classes."

Ricardo, a nine-year-old homeschooler from Chapel Hill, North Carolina, echoed this sentiment in an interview with me:

> I have more time with my friends now than
> when I was in school. In school, even though they

51

kind of wanted you to make friends, you didn't
really have that time with your friends, like you
could get in trouble for talking with your friends
instead of working. After school you have to do
like an hour of homework, and then you usually
eat dinner and go to bed. Now we have time to
play with our friends when we come to the
[homeschool] play dates or when we go to their
house or they come to our house.—*Ricardo, nine-
year-old homeschooler, Chapel Hill, NC*

Marena, a ten-year-old homeschooler, shares her
perspective:

Maybe when you're in school, you can't really
play with [your friends]. If you get yelled at for
talking in class, or something like that, you can't
really talk to them or play with them. In [our
homeschool group] you can really talk and do
whatever you want, whenever, unless your mom
wants you to do something else, you know. I like
being able to have friends who are available a lot.
... It's nice to be—to feel—free.—*Marena,
homeschooled ten-year-old, Durham, NC*

And parents question the social value of peer
contact in school as well:

Socialization: this is something that
everybody asked me about. I would say, "You don't
understand. Being homeschooled doesn't mean
that you don't spend time with other children."
When you look at a classroom situation, it's very
controlled. What opportunity do children have to
socialize? Only recess, which is about fifteen
minutes a day, and lunch. If that's the kind of
socialization that's available, I'm not interested.
School kids get socialization by playing after
school, joining groups like Cub Scouts, [and so on],
the same way homeschoolers do. It's not like

homeschoolers never see another child. I just don't understand where that comes from.

Don't they understand that this is part of education, too? It's more than reading, writing, and arithmetic. It's how you behave towards other people.—*Norma, homeschooling mother, Big Flats, NY*

Socializing in a Homeschool Lifestyle

The reality is that homeschoolers have a great deal of time to interact and play with peers, since academic work, in whatever form it takes, is much more efficient in a homeschool, leaving a majority of time for social and other activities. Many families do not even separate academic work from other aspects of life at all, instead combining real-life learning experiences with social life.

In fact, many children who have spent time in both homeschool and conventional school say they have not only more time with friends, but also closer friends while homeschooling than they did in school.

Sebastien, a twelve-year-old, was homeschooled for three years and now attends school. Here are his observations on some differences (names and some identifying details in the following account have been changed):

I liked homeschooling a lot better than school. It was a lot better because my mom knew me and how I learned, so she was able to help me learn the way I learn.

It also gave me a lot more free time because you can hurry up and finish, and you don't have to wait for everyone else to finish. And when you're done, you can get up and go. Not like in school, where when you're done, you have to wait for everyone else.

I had friends in my sports activities. I had lots of friends. All the kids that I played sports with were homeschooled. I had more closer friends before, when I was homeschooled. Now, in school, there are friends, but not as close.—*Sebastien, twelve-year-old, formerly homeschooled for three years.*

Sebastien's mother, Angela, adds her perspective:
I think that he has so many experiences that most children won't have, especially because he was in homeschool sports. He was with a group of homeschoolers, and they were together all day, all weekend—you know, they were very, very close. They had a lot of sleepovers, and we traveled together, so they became very close friends. We did a lot that conventionally schooled kids wouldn't do. So he was happier, but at the same time, he was doing what he needed to do just to develop. So I think he had more experiences that he'll never forget while he was homeschooling. —*Angela, former homeschooling mother of two*

And other parents notice this, too:
[My thirteen-year-old daughter] has a lot more good friends now—true friends who are kind to her and care about her—than she ever did in school.—*Montie, homeschooling mother of one, Alamance, NC*

Homeschoolers get real-life, down-to-earth, meaningful interactions with diverse people on a daily basis. They build friendships, resolve conflicts, make decisions for themselves, and seek guidance from their parents at a time in their lives when learning about people, relationships, and the world is needed not going it alone or clinging desperately to peers for guidance and hoping for the best.

One mother shares how her daughter has had a more positive social experience through homeschooling:

She spends way more time with friends now than she ever did when she was in school, unless you count sitting in a classroom next to twenty other kids as social time, but I don't. When she was in school, she would occasionally have people over and she would certainly play with kids nearby in the neighborhood, but now she's not limited to weekends or the time span between 3:00 and 7:00 at night that she can see her friends. So I think she spends a lot more time with kids her own age now than she ever did in school—really spending time, not just sitting in a classroom. She has friends over, and they can take several hours and go to the park. ... I don't have to engineer their playtime, there doesn't have to be a design around the time. I see that as a benefit. So does homeschooling detrimentally affect her ability to form relationships with other people or time with friends? No is the answer to that because she's got more time with friends. There's only been good effects on that.—*Christine, homeschooling mother of one, Durham, NC*

Peer Contact vs. Peer Dependence

With that said, the assumption that a large quantity of random peer interaction is necessary or even healthy is just that—an assumption—and may be unfounded in the first place. It certainly seems to be a commonly held belief in this culture (a culture comprised of people raised in schools) that quantity of peer interaction is a—if not the—key factor in children's socialization. But other than popular belief, do we have any evidence that this is so? Patricia M. Lines, in the Educational Resources Information Center (ERIC) Digest, claims that homeschooled kids spend less time with peers and more time with people from different age groups (but does not substantiate this claim); still later she admits that no conclusive research supports the idea that more time with peers in a child's own age group is preferable over more time with people of a variety of ages (Lines 2001).

In fact, psychologists suggest that what we often think of as socialization with peers is actually peer dependence. It could be argued that an unnaturally large quantity of essentially random exposure to and interaction with peers (as found in schools), when not balanced with adequate contact, guidance, and relationship with friendly adults, is unhealthy and part of "the problem." Certainly it is debatable whether the current system is socializing children into healthy adults, considering the rates of divorce, crime, suicide, alcoholism, drug abuse, and so on as they are today.

This is not to say that kids do not need plenty of peer contact. In all likelihood, they do need to play with friends and not rely on their parents (or even siblings) to be their sole playmates. However, there is no evidence that playing all day with two or three close friends is in any way inferior for children socially than spending the days passing in and out of the lives of large numbers of miscellaneous peers.

Kids need role models and learn through imitation and emulation. By staying close (physically and emotionally) to their parents, children have the opportunity to observe their parents' friendships and social interactions and model their own social behavior after that of their older, more experienced parents rather than after that of other young children who are only "beginners" like themselves. Through homeschooling, kids have time for both plentiful peer contact and this healthy parental proximity.

A Few Friends vs.
Many Acquaintances

Homeschoolers relate again and again that they do have fewer acquaintances but more close friends than they would have (or had) in school. And they often cite this as an advantage of homeschooling, as this fifteen-year-old does:

> For fun, I like to cycle with my friends a lot. We go out on the lake and have talks about whatever, all sorts of things. I feel like I have fewer acquaintances and more true friends who would stick with me through hard times. Those are the friends who really count: the ones who actually care about you.
>
> There's really not too much I dislike [about homeschooling].—*Julian, fifteen-year-old homeschooler, Katonah, NY*

Indeed, though some amount of peer contact is undoubtedly important and healthy, it is only in recent history that peers have filled so many roles for each other. Just as adults do not necessarily make ideal primary playmates for children, neither do children usually serve well as each other's primary role models or social mentors. When peers begin to take the place of experienced role models, wise mentors, and responsible authority figures, such peer contact ceases to be healthy and becomes instead a problem. David Guterson, in his book *Family Matters: Why Home Schooling Makes Sense*, points out that mass schooling essentially separates adults from kids, placing them in a position of absolute authority over many kids at once in a way that essentially precludes the formation of meaningful adult-child relationships. "Their need for adults, unfulfilled and frustrated, urges them to grasp even more obsessively—this is a staple of psychological theory about adolescent peer dependency—at what their peers have to offer in consolation" (Guterson 1992).

Homeschooling does not seem to produce this same effect. Delahooke (1986) found that homeschooled kids were less peer-dependent than private school students (the researcher didn't study public school kids) (NHERI 2003). And homeschoolers consider this lack of peer dependence a boon:

> Bottom line: It doesn't really matter what your kids learn, as long as they get a positive socialization experience. If you can be the greatest [note that she does not say "only"—R.G.] influence in their lives, [that's how it's done.] Peer dependence can only hurt that, not help it. That's what homeschoolers have found.—Audrey, homeschooling mother of ten, Garner, NC

> Do I think that it's necessary for kids in general to spend lots of time with peers? No. I don't think there's like X amount of time a day or a week that you should spend with people your same age. I can honestly say that my two kids don't even particularly ask for that. It's not like they wake up in the morning and say, "Who are we playing with today?" because they play so much with each other.—*Ann, homeschooling mother of two, Chapel Hill, NC*

Is All Peer Contact Equal?

In her book *Home Schooling*, Lee Stewart describes a day that clarified the issue of peer contact at school for her. When her children were in school, she had considered homeschooling but was too concerned about socialization in the form of peer contact to pursue it. One day she happened to visit the school and observed the behavior of the children toward one another during an extended recess-type situation. She observed exclusiveness, violence, and unfriendliness and discussed her concern with the adults in charge, who seemed unconcerned about these behaviors. "I came to the conclusion that day," she says, "that the social contact which I was so concerned about was 95 percent negative. Our children could do better without it." Indeed, once her children began homeschooling, she says, they became more friendly and self-confident and found it easier to socialize with both children and adults (Stewart 1990).

Grace Llewellyn, who shares observations of many teenaged homeschoolers in her book *The Teenage Liberation Handbook*, echoes this, observing that homeschoolers don't have as many acquaintances but "develop stronger, closer friendships. They appreciate not having to spend time with hordes of people they don't have a lot in common with" (Llewellyn 1998).

And other real-life homeschoolers agree. Jane, a Minnesota homeschooling mother of a thirteen-year-old and an eleven-year-old, has this to say:

> The logic of throwing a kid into an environment with other kids who have been selected by no other criterion than that they are the same age defies me. Homeschooling allows kids to select their social network in a fashion similar to that they'll use for the rest of their lives. My kids select their friends because they have similar interests and goals first, not because they're the same age and have desirable labels on their clothes.—*Jane, homeschooling mother of two, Minnesota*

James, a homeschooling father, adds his experience:

> [My wife's] big worry was, "There's no

friends." You know, there's no one to invite to birthday parties and there's nobody to do anything. So a year ago or so, I'm like, "Well okay, we'll go get involved in something [that is, a homeschooling group]." And now I can't—there's too much. They've got too many friends! They've got too many people. [We] just spend every day out visiting; Monday it's down at Indian Trail [Park], Thursday it's the actual [homeschool play date] event, Friday who knows where we [are]. ... I've got people from their soccer league calling—there are so many kids their age, and other ages, it's ridiculous.

I think when [my son] was in school, he had a group of friends. ... He had probably more people that he was with a lot, but I don't think he felt like he really belonged. He had a couple of people that were his friends, but nobody that was like, "Hey, come over here; let's go do this thing." He was just thrown into those people because they were all the same age, right? I mean in the school situation, they go in and they basically interact all day with kids who—why are they there? Again, they were born in the same period of time. All those nine-year-olds or seven-year-olds or whatever are all from the same geographic region, so they have all of that in common, whereas my kids get that, get people at the museums, get all the parents that they interact with daily at the homeschool groups, you know. I don't know that they necessarily interact with more people, but they have the option to.—*James, homeschooling father of three, Durham, NC*

Homeschooled kids notice a difference in the quality of their social interaction, too:

When you're in school, there are people who pick on other people, and I was the one who got picked on, so I didn't like school very much. Say you're wearing pink socks: They make you think that they hate pink, so they're like, "Okay, Chelsea, you've got stupid socks," and things like that basically to tear the other person down and make [themselves] feel better.

But homeschooling's fun. That doesn't happen in homeschooling.

Like me and [my friend], we know what it's like to be in school, and I guess when you're homeschooled you care more about their feelings, so you don't pick on them. Me and my mom think that it's because you're being taught by your mom 24/7, instead of some lady that's paid to teach you.

So you've got more [moms who] teach you more—like not to pick on people—more guidance. But when you're in school, there's nobody teaching you how to act; they just teach you writing and math and so on. I remember [when I was in school] people weren't very nice, and I only had one friend. They picked on me because, well, I think they picked on me because I have a good life. I have my mom, I have a dad, I have two brothers.

I didn't like it there. I'd rather homeschool. —*Chelsea, eleven-year-old homeschooler, Efland, NC*

I'm thirteen and have been homeschooling since I was about ten or eleven. Before that I went to a public magnet school, about 360 kids. I started homeschooling a few months before the end of fifth grade because I got impatient with the lack of teaching time, the overabundance of discipline time, and kids being jerks, basically. Everybody was nasty to each other, but also to me in particular because I was not in any of the cliques. So they were picking on me, and I got tired of it and left.

I find homeschooling very, very different. For one thing, people actually seem to like me.—*Brit, thirteen-year-old homeschooler, Durham, NC*

Parents comment, too, that for some reason, homeschooling seems to encourage more positive social behavior in children. One mother, Ann, adds:

> I do find her homeschool friends, on the whole, just a kinder group of people, less likely to maybe point out things that are superficial or different, like what you're wearing. I see the difference with her friends now who are still in school. I didn't see it [when she went to school] in kindergarten, you know—they were all a kinder group with each other. Now I'm starting to see a big difference. She's still friends with kids who go to school, but I just see her [homeschool] friends as so much kinder. They're kind people.—*Ann, homeschooling mother of two, Chapel Hill, NC*

Christine, mother of one, tells about social changes she noticed in addition to her daughter having more time with friends:

> Her friends—well, not really her friends but her classmates [at school]—were saying things to her that made her feel like there was something wrong with who she was. I'm trying to remember an example. That she talked too much, they would call her names: jabbermouth, bigmouth. Oh, [they would call her] fat. (Second grade!) Stuff like that. She was not happy, and I was not happy.
>
> Our reasons now [for homeschooling] are that we really love it, because [my daughter] has the freedom to learn about what she wants to learn about in the way that she feels most comfortable learning about it. She is relatively free from the social pressures that she was under at school. She doesn't have to deal with being made fun of. She does have to deal with it a little bit, but not in a classroom situation every day or anything like that. Her friends are real friends in that they're accepting of her the way she is, and they aren't

trying to mold her into something that she's not.
—*Christine, homeschooling mother of one,
Durham, NC*

Certainly many school-going children are also very kind and treat each other well. This is in no way meant to suggest that schoolchildren are "not nice." Still, homeschoolers consistently relate the observation that, for some reason, homeschooled children do not seem as inclined to "pick on" each other or engage in "mean" behavior. Children who leave school and become homeschoolers often express relief at finding that, for whatever reason, they are no longer ridiculed or pressured to be something they are not.

Different-Aged Peers

In addition to getting contact and quality interaction with same-aged peers, homeschoolers also get another important kind of social opportunity: friendships with children (and adults) of a wide range of ages. When I interviewed homeschoolers across the United States and Canada and asked them what they liked about homeschooling, I was surprised to discover that many of the kids I talked to cited getting to have a wider variety of friends, especially different age groups, as a favorite aspect. This came up so often that I am going to quote several of them:

> [I like being around] people my own age and other ages. [In school] several of my friends were older or younger than me, and I didn't get to see them, except occasionally we'd get to wave at each other in the hallways when our little lines passed each other. Schools never seem to approve of the mixing of different age groups, and I love the mixing of different age groups. I think segregation of the different age groups is very stupid, especially

if you're trying to prepare us for jobs because in jobs you're literally never going to work in a group of say, twenty-three-year-olds; you're going to work in a group with twenty-three-year-olds, fifty-year-olds, eighty-year-olds, anything. So it's not teaching us to interact with any other age groups than our own.

I love homeschooling. I recognize homeschooling is not for every kid, not for every family, not everyone can do it, but public schooling and private schooling is not for every kid or every family either. It all depends on who you're thinking about. I wouldn't say that public schooling is bad for all children, and I wouldn't say that homeschooling is good for all children. I'm just saying that public schooling's bad for me, and homeschooling's really good for me.

I really like my social life. I have met a lot of people. At [our homeschool group's] play dates, you don't have to just talk to your friends—usually you do, but you can talk to anybody: the adults, the little kids, anyone. I've always loved little kids, so I don't like being separated from them. I'm around lots of very different kinds of people because I'm in several different homeschooling groups and I do different things with each of them. That is something that's important to me, because in general, diversity is the spice of life. I like to be around lots of different people.—*Brit, thirteen-year-old homeschooler, Durham, NC*

I like how you're not all in a group with the same age as you—like me and [a fifteen-year-old friend of mine]. I'd never be able to be friends with someone much older than me [in school]. —*Haleigh, nine-year-old homeschooler, Chapel Hill, NC*

> At school you don't really hang out with the people who are older than you—you hang out with the people in your class, or the people that you see at recess.—*Chelsea, eleven-year-old homeschooler, Efland, NC*

And the parents commented on this frequently as well. Angela, the former homeschooling mother of two, says (names and some identifying details in the following account have been changed):

> Not only are they socializing with the kids in their classes, they're socializing with adults and children of all ages. My son was in sports all day. He was six years old, and the oldest was fifteen. And they were all together, all day long. It had boys, it had girls, plus their coaches, so they were socializing all day. And I know plenty of people who have children of all ages, and they go to their homeschooling group and socialize with people of all different ages. So they get along with more children, not just with the kids their age. And the peer pressure's not as significant when they're homeschooling. They don't have to conform to what is popular in school.—*Angela, former homeschooling mother of two*

Catherine, a mother with three homeschooling kids, says:

> Oh yeah, [my kids associate with] many more age groups. They'll talk to kids older and younger, they'll talk to adults more, and ... they talk to all different-aged kids that they wouldn't have. They talk to the parents of those kids that they normally wouldn't have. They were really shy—they wouldn't talk to anyone before they started homeschooling. If an adult was talking to me and then talked to them, they would turn their face away. So afraid to face them, they just didn't even

want to see that they were there. Totally shy, and that's gone. It seems to be because of homeschooling. It seemed to go away completely when that started. I don't know why.

I can pick out homeschooled kids when they come for eye exams just by the way they talk to me. It's like it's an adult-to-adult conversation, and it's just easier to talk to them. The school kids—they answer yes or no if they absolutely have to. One of the kids a few weeks ago just wouldn't say anything. I kept asking him to read the letters, and he just sat there silently and wouldn't do it. Finally, by the end he would do it, after I asked him about five times. And actually I picked out a homeschool parent the other day, and she didn't even have her kids with her. I said, "Do you homeschool your kids?" and she said, "Yes." I don't know why that happens. There's just something about them that I can pick them out. With the kids I'm pretty sure it's the way they talk to me. We can have a conversation, and they'll have fun.—*Catherine, homeschooling mother of three, Durham, NC*

Another parent adds:

Socially, [my son] can hold a conversation with anyone. We have received many comments, such as, "What a polite young man" and "He's only five? He's quite a talker." I also notice that he's not afraid to help out children who are younger than him. For instance, one day we were at the park meeting with other homeschoolers from our area—as we do each week in the spring, summer, and fall months—and he noticed a little girl getting pushed and bumped by the older kids. He went over to this little girl, took her hand, and brought her closer to her mother. He then started to play with her on the climbers. They were

pretending it was a ship, and he showed her how
to turn the steering wheel and make a ship sound.
I would say the little girl couldn't have been any
older than two. The mother later told me I have a
very compassionate little boy. I thanked her.

[My son] has about fourteen cousins of
different ages (my husband has a large family),
and he has no problem playing their games or
talking with them. Most of them are happy to play
in his imagination games, too. So we have plenty
of opportunity for socialization.—*Theresa,
homeschooling mother of one, Ontario, Canada*

Parents also frequently relate observations on how
their kids benefit socially from interacting with a more
diverse age range:

I especially like that benefit of
homeschooling: the fact that the children learn to
relate to all age groups, not just their own class.

When they socialize with different age
groups, they seem to be more comfortable in a
variety of situations. They seem more confident
across the board. The homeschooling group we are
involved in, the Outdoor Learning Project, has
children from two to seventeen. They all interact
and work together on various "classroom" projects
and in exploring the outdoors.

I think the kids need exposure to all age
groups. There is lots to learn from others, and they
can gain valuable experience in sharing what they
know, too. Even reading a story to a younger child
is a valuable experience. The real world is
composed of all age groups. I think that keeping
kids in a group of other kids all the same age might
keep them from learning some of those skills.
—*Susan, homeschooling mother of two,
Orangeville, Ontario*

One thing that people often said about [my kids] was they were so polite, so respectful, and that they knew how to talk to people who weren't their same age. I put a lot of that down to the fact that they had the influence at home rather than at school. [One thing that] we have found is that our kids could talk to anyone, not just another eight-year-old. They were always comfortable with younger kids and older people. You need connections with both ends of the spectrum. I don't think they lost anything at all by homeschooling.
—*Norma, homeschooling mother, Big Flats, New York*

Is [socialization] a drawback to the homeschooler? Definitely not. I would say that homeschool kids have the advantage when it comes to socialization opportunities. There are so many things to do around town, to get our kids interested in, and to get them to meet other homeschoolers. Most of these things are done with a wide range of age variance.

Most homeschooling children do not experience the same things as kids from the public school: peer pressure or discrimination (age, gender, religion, or race). In my opinion, homeschool kids learn, on their own, that it is okay to play with any child. In school I believe the opposite is taught. [In homeschooling] there is not a big focus on what the age or the gender the child is before deciding if they "should" play with that child. I have met several families that pulled their children out of public school, just on this issue alone. It can be devastating to a child.

In homeschooling environments I have observed an older homeschooled child coming to the assistance of a younger child when there were difficulties, or just to lend a helping hand.

Homeschooling kids learn to socialize in a more natural way. In life there is no such thing as all thirty-five-year-olds working together or only girls at the office. In school, I would imagine, that might be the impression children get.

My four-year-old feels comfortable and accomplished when he can participate in an experiment with his older siblings. My oldest is not intimidated by the fact that his younger sister (by twenty months) is learning at a faster pace than him. In fact, he sometimes takes lessons from her—rather than mom!—*Suzanne, homeschooling mother of three, Scottsdale, AZ*

Freedom to Have Solitude

In all the discussion about children's need for peer contact, another important need is sometimes overlooked: the need for solitude. For many homeschooled children and families, the freedom to stay home, have solitude, and introspect when feeling withdrawn or needing "down" time is a great boon of homeschooling. Especially for a more introverted child, the ability to listen to his needs and spend more time alone or with family, or perhaps with one close friend, is particularly important. Homeschooling affords families the liberty to vary social settings, spending some days in large groups, others in smaller groups, some with one or two close friends, and some in privacy or with family, rather than spending every day in the same social setting (that is, a large group of peers).

One homeschooling mother shares how her family spends their time:

He does a lot of creative things, a lot of creative play by himself. He recharges himself, and he's introverted, so he's gonna be drained by being around a lot of people. He gets energized and motivated and does a lot of his creative stuff on his own, either one on one with a friend or one on one with my husband or the three of us or by himself completely.—*Missy, homeschooling mother of two, Cary, NC*

Some days parents and children need "home days," and with homeschooling, they can take them. Homeschoolers can respond to their personal needs without learning to feel guilty about doing so or to value the system more than they value their own needs or temperaments. In the "real world" of adulthood, those who prefer to work alone or in smaller groups are not forced to live and work in large group settings without personal days, but are free to pursue jobs or careers that fit their individual temperaments. Extroverts, or those who prefer or need to be around many people, are likewise free to pursue situations suitable for them. Homeschooling allows this self-discovery to happen naturally and comfortably, thus preparing children to find future situations suitable to their needs.

The reality of homeschooling is that it affords children plenty of peer contact, as well as the safety, guidance, and social learning provided by parental proximity. Perhaps it is this safety and guidance that contributes to the higher quality of social relationships that homeschoolers seem to enjoy.

But is so much time with parents good for kids? Don't kids need to be with their friends without their parents around in order to learn independence and have a true social life? In the next chapter, we will explore whether this is so and to what extent kids need to be with or away from parents. We will examine whether the increased amount of time parents spend with their children while homeschooling is helpful and healthy for children and hear directly from the source how it affects many homeschoolers.

chapter five

INDEPENDENCE AND STRONG FAMILY RELATIONSHIPS

"The basic quality of our emotional maturity, we now realize, is largely the result of the relationship between parent and child."—Alan Fromme, Ph.D.

"The family that plays together stays together."
—Unknown

In preparation for this book, I interviewed homeschooling parents and kids from all over the US and Canada about their reasons for homeschooling and the effects it has had on their lives. I interviewed homeschoolers of all ages, backgrounds, and family types. Everyone had a different story to share, but there was one common theme that I heard again and again from family after family: that the biggest advantages they had experienced, and the most important aspects of homeschooling to them, are the time they get to spend together and the effects it has had on their family relationships.

Throughout this book, homeschoolers share many different stories, many approaches to homeschooling, and many reasons for doing it, but through all of them runs this one common thread: time with family.

This is because of one of the great unknown truths about homeschooling: the increased time homeschoolers experience with parents and family is a benefit to children socially and prepares and strengthens them for future relationships and social situations.

"Can't Let Go?"

Critics of homeschooling sometimes assert that children need to be separated from their parents in order to learn independence and experience things they would not (or would not be allowed to) if their parents were around. They worry that children may be stifled by their parents' presence.

David Guterson sums up this concern well: "Their assumption is that the intimacy between parent and child inherent in the homeschooling life is potentially obsessive, unhealthy, sentimental, perhaps even dangerous to the child's developing psyche. They worry that as social beings our [kids] will strangle under the weight of our relentless presence, birdlings never pushed from the nest, so to speak, and forever limited—perhaps forever neurotic too—as a consequence" (Guterson 1992). Onlookers may wonder: is the parent just having trouble letting go, afraid to allow the child any freedom to grow and become an independent individual?

Homeschooling parents have thoughtful and fascinating answers to these questions, beginning with two basic assertions: one, yes, we can, and do, let go—homeschooling does not mean our kids spend as much time around us as you might imagine; and two, parents are not supposed to let go as early as popular culture gives us to believe—kids need us, and that is why they have parents. Interestingly, these two seemingly contradictory answers often come from the same parents, and we will soon see why.

Do Homeschooled Children Have Time Away From Their Parents?

The simple answer is yes, homeschool kids do spend time away. Contrary to popular image, they are not always with their parents. Like other kids, they go over to friends' houses, play with neighborhood kids, talk on the phone, go to summer camp and extracurricular classes, join sports teams, ride their bikes at the park, go to movies, get babysat, babysit, go to the mall, and when they're old enough, date. They experience peer interactions of all kinds, with both conventionally schooled children and other homeschoolers.

In fact, even when the parents and children are together, many homeschooling parents are careful to stay out of the child's way as much as possible, not stifling but quietly supervising from the background. Many homeschoolers believe, like the late renowned educator Charlotte Mason, that "the part of the mother or teacher in the early years (indeed, all through life) is to sow opportunities, and then to keep in the background, ready with a guiding or restraining hand only when these are badly wanted" (Mason 1993).

Two homeschoolers share their experiences:

> So [my daughter] had been going off to Raleigh to dance classes and was having to take the bus to get there. That's what she needed to do, and once we figured out that she could do it,

she did it. The limitation has really been the fact that we live where you pretty much have to drive where you want to go, and so that's boxed them in the way that suburban lifestyle does.... But last year in St. Louis we weren't living that way, and [my other daughter] got herself around. Then also they've always gotten themselves around by making arrangements with friends to pick them up and take them where they wanted to go.—*Sarah, homeschooling mother of four, Durham, NC*

My parents have given me a *lot* of freedom. And they have given me the opportunity to pursue the things I love, such as snowboarding and cycling, which I am considering pursuing as a career, and they really support me wholeheartedly in that. I've always had the freedom I want, and that's always been the best thing for me [about homeschooling]. It's great to be able to do the things I want to do.—*Julian, fifteen-year-old homeschooler, Katonah, NY*

Yes, homeschoolers do get time away from their parents. But with that said, the question arises as to how important this time away really is.

Parents and Family Time

There is another issue that ultimately may be far more important. Research has indicated that the most important aspect of socialization is not relationships with peers, but relationships with adults (Bunday 1999). And, of course, this is nothing new. It has long been known that parental involvement is the number one factor in kids' success at school, and it is likewise in the family that the most important social learning occurs. All types of educators and school personnel agree that the most important social and other learning occurs at home. And needless to say, parental involvement is a defining element of homeschooling.

There is plenty of evidence that kids need lots of time *with* parents, but is there any evidence that they need any particular amount of time away? Or is this just a cultural myth?

The idea that early and abundant independence from parents is desirable may be part of an overall societal pressure on kids and parents toward early, forced independence (also seen in pressures toward early weaning, sleeping alone and through the night at a very young age, and so forth). More and more research is showing, and parents are discovering, that strong attachment bonds between child and parents, not forced independence, creates happy children and healthy socialization.

The idea that the kids need freedom from their parents at a young age seems based on the premise that parents are a "crutch," to be cast aside as soon as physically possible. However, many homeschoolers believe that children need their parents directly available to them for much more of their childhoods than conventional schooling allows. They want to teach their children what they consider to be healthy social skills, rather than send them to learn whatever skills they might happen to learn from their peers. And they want themselves and their children to experience the closer family relationships that homeschooling seems to encourage:

> I honestly could not imagine sending my children off to school. After planning home births, breastfeeding, and [having] a genuine love for my time with my children, it seemed wrong to place such a huge part of their lives in someone else's hands. Maybe that was a little selfish on my part, not letting them go off to school, but they are very happy to be learning at home. ... I am a firm

believer in life skills. Children need more family time these days!

The benefits are enormous. My children enjoy each other's company (most days; sometimes we all need a break to refresh). ... Their outlook on life astounds me at times (we live for the moment). They have taught me many things over the years, and we enjoy learning together.
—*Pamela, mother of four, Port Hope, Ontario*

[My daughter] went till third grade in public school, and [my son] went till fifth grade. Now they're in sixth and seventh respectively. I started homeschooling for a couple of reasons. Initially, [my daughter] started having a hard time. She doesn't work that well with the curriculum that's chosen in public school. Then on top of that, she was having problems socially. She was picked on really bad. ... At the same time, [my son] was in fourth grade, and the boys were starting to do this macho, competitive thing and turning into jerks. His behavior and social skills and all that stuff were starting to go. I didn't like the person he started to act like, and then [my daughter] was reacting to being picked on by being [ornery]. In fact, I started to go, "Wow, I wonder if these [expletive deleted] women that you see are really little girls who were attacked for whatever reason when they were little and they reacted by building up walls and being abrasive themselves." So I decided to pull them out.

After I decided to pull them out, though, I read books, went to conventions, and discovered that they belonged with me anyways and that I had missed many years. My relationship with them was lacking in huge ways, and I was going to spend the rest of the time rebuilding what I was [missing]. So even though I did it for the social reasons and the school curriculum not working and all, I eventually realized that it was more about the fact that they belonged at home with me. Now I just realize that no matter how good the school was or no matter how bad the situation was—whether it was a bad teacher or bad curriculum—that it doesn't matter what the curriculum is, what the structure is, or socially what's going on. Everybody could be perfectly nice, and I would still want them at home. Some people think that I would send them to a private school if I could afford to, but I wouldn't. I wouldn't send them anywhere. And I want them to stay home until they go to college. People go, "What are you going to do for high school?" and I go, "Well, I'm gonna teach them all the way to college."

[The differences in our family relationships are] huge. Huge. Huge, the way that we interact, how much time I have to listen to the children, how much time I have to answer the important questions that come up at odd times, how the kids interact, how calm I am, how much fighting there is in the family—you know, their social skills are growing, their friends are growing, they're learning how to communicate … it's huge. It's all about the time we spend together.—*Rachel, homeschooling mother of three, Hillsborough, NC*

Allies

And, given the chance, homeschooled kids express that, on the whole, they do like to have their parents (and siblings) around and appreciate having close relationships with them. The strong family relationships that homeschooling facilitates make it easier for all family members to enjoy being around each other:

One thing that changed a lot when [my daughter] came home from school was just an ease in our own relationship. We just like to be together, and I find her an interesting person. ... It just got so much easier than when I was having to get her out of bed way too early in the morning and she was grumpy and cold and not wanting to be awake. Then when picking her up from school she was more grumpy and more out of sorts and just kind of de-programming and de-stressing from the day—it seems like that was mostly our relationship when she was in school. And now we have a really easy relationship. We like to be together, we like to spend time together. What she will ask me more often than being with peers is can WE do something together. "Mom, can we have a girl's day?" She asks for that pretty regularly. And we get to do that pretty often. The boys have a boy's day, and the girls have a girl's day at our house, and it's good.

I just feel like our whole life is so much more nourishing in each and every way. The way our family is together and the way we celebrate the seasons together, and it just all weaves together. We have this life now, where before we had more of an existence I would say, and a lot of shuttling here and there, maintenancey-type activities, you know. Now it's time to get dressed, now it's time to do this ... and now it's just like we have this— we just have this life—I don't know how to describe it.—*Ann, homeschooling mother of two, Chapel Hill, NC*

Kids I spoke to also told me again and again that they like having more time with their parents:

I'm around my mom more now than when I was in school. I think I spend a lot more time with my mom and my stepfather. ... I spend more time with them, and I like it that way because

78

sometimes [before] it would just be like I would be in school and I was just so sick of the same things every single day. Now, since I have the rest of the day, I'm not doing the same old same old every single day. I have more time to actually do things with my mother—and just being normal with my mother—instead of just having to plot time out of your same old on-the-same-track-every-day life to see your own mom. Because [when I was in school], all the time I spent with my mother was asking her questions about my math homework.—*Corrin, eleven-year-old homeschooler, Durham, NC*

People my age will say to me, "I can't believe you have to spend so much time with your parents! How can you stand it? That's horrible, I would hate that." But I like being around my parents. I'm not saying we didn't have our disputes, but homeschooling brought me *much* closer to them. Most of my school friends, once they were eighteen, couldn't wait to get out of the house and get as far away as they could from home. For me it was the opposite: I thought, "I don't want to leave yet." I am applying to colleges, and I am ready to leave home and move out and on, but I don't feel a need to "escape" from home. It's not restricting being at home; I have all the freedom I need. I just don't feel any restriction or pressure from [my parents].

A similar thing happens with drinking and smoking and stuff. Why didn't I want to rebel? I don't know. I just never did. [My parents] weren't rabid about things; they just lived that way, and I grew to agree with them.—*Stephanie, eighteen-year-old college student, homeschooled until college, Katonah, NY*

I think I was definitely around my parents more than a lot of people who go to school are. I

79

can say that for sure. Because I wasn't away for those hours every day, and I didn't have homework to keep me distracted in the evenings, so there's definitely a lot more social interaction within my family that I think a lot of people didn't have— which for me was a good thing. I think a lot of people, a lot of my peers, would think about homeschooling and the first thing they'd think about is how awful it would be to have to be with their family that much. I didn't feel that way. I was accustomed to it, and I get along well with my family. And so it's just something I don't consider remarkable.

I think overall I had a positive social experience with my family, my friends, and both combined. They've probably taught me a lot more than I ever suspected they did at the time. I've probably learned a lot from them that I wasn't aware I was learning *from them*, just by being in their presence and listening to their conversations and by having conversations with them. They rarely took the role of teacher in the sense of "lecturer," but certainly they were great educational resources if I ever had any questions about anything.

I considered them my allies.—*David, nineteen-year-old, homeschooled since birth, Durham, NC*

On the other hand, as kids *do* reach an age when they can handle and need greater independence, homeschool parents—who have already spent a great deal of time with their kids—are generally very willing to give them a healthily increasing amount of freedom and independence.

Elizabeth, the mother of a pre-teen, relates her observations of her daughter's growing up and her own reactions to it:

She's eleven. It was this standing up to—not really defiant, but sort of an assertiveness. Separation, that's it. That's what I really notice. Before it was, "You're my mommy, and I love you and never want to leave you. Half my identity is tied up in you." And now it's, "I'm me, you're you."

I kind of saw myself when they were born as, "It's my job to raise them and get them that way." So if I can get them to be independent, grown-up people, I'm really proud of that. I always wanted independent [individuals]. ... I never babied them; I didn't talk baby talk.—*Elizabeth, homeschooling mother of two, Raleigh, NC*

Another mother relates her experience as well:

My kids are twenty-one, nineteen, sixteen, and thirteen years old. They've always had as much freedom as they wanted. I know when they need more freedom or independence because they just take it.

I actually had several conversations with [my daughter], ... and I several times told her specifically that going to college was not the only way to leave home.—*Sarah, homeschooling mother of four (two grown up), Durham, NC*

And homeschooling experts have observed this as well. David Guterson, in his book *Family Matters: Why Homeschooling Makes Sense*, notes, "Homeschooling parents never worry about 'quality time' and are thus well able, many of them, to let go of their children at an early age, when their children need this letting go" (Guterson 1992). Grace Llewellyn, author of the *Teenage Liberation Handbook*, says, "In general, unschooling allows teenagers to stay 'young' as long as they want, but also to 'grow up' as soon as they are ready" (Llewellyn 1998).

A homeschooled childhood is, in many ways,

different from a schooled one. Homeschooling generally does not seem to result in kids feeling alienated from adults the way conventional schooling tends to. Kids who are not required by their parents to go to school on a daily basis, like it or not—kids of parents who are themselves taking a risk by going against the grain to spare their kids what they consider a less desirable experience—may and often do view their parents as allies rather than as wardens to rebel against. The kids know that their parents have chosen to spend this time (which they could easily have free by enrolling the kids in public school) with them. Rearing and living with children can be difficult. It can be even more difficult when families' time together is concentrated around the stressful, tired hours at the end of the day when everybody is drained or scrambling to get homework done, eat dinner, and get to bed. When parents are able to spend more time with their children, they have a chance to get the "good hours," too, and often find that they and their kids learn how better to interact and be with one another. When this happens, it becomes a joy to spend days together, and kids get the gift of parents who enjoy them.

But the question of whether a child "should" like her parents so much is a source of controversy in and of itself. Sometimes liking one's parents is actually viewed as a sign of inadequate socialization, and this may be the result of years of indoctrination in which we, as a culture, have come to view authority figures (on some level) as the "enemy" and to believe that it is right and best to feel this way. However, it may in actuality be healthier to grow up trusting and liking our authority figures, especially when those figures are benevolent, caring, and acting in our best interests. (Homeschoolers' relationship with adults and authority will be explored in greater depth in Chapter 9.)

In a typical schooling lifestyle—one in which each family member leads essentially his own separate life, runs in his own circle, and has his own totally separate group of friends—parents and children must often be away from their friends and their individual "lives" in order to spend time together. Under these circumstances, it follows naturally and understandably that children often come to view spending time with their parents as a chore—something "boring," "lame," or even embarrassing. With homeschooling, children do not seem as prone to feel this way, since spending time with their parents and spending time with their friends often happen simultaneously. In many cases, the children are able to socialize with friends while parents remain available to them nearby, something the children often appreciate. Since most of us associate time with parents as meaning time away from friends, non-homeschoolers may understandably imagine the homeschooling life to be one lacking in peer contact.

And the family unity that homeschoolers are so grateful for actually enables kids to have more (and higher quality) time with their friends.

James, father of three, says:

> There were at least forty-five or fifty families that we theoretically ran into in [our kids' school] classes, and we were never connected in a way at all with any of them, which absolutely amazed me.
>
> There's absolutely no doubt in my mind that that translates directly into the social life of the kids. Even that is huge. When your kids have a social life and you have a social life, they're two separate things. [In school] my kids have this group of friends that are their classmates, and I have this group of parents that I've met through work or whatever that are in common with us.

[My kids] know nothing about my friends, and I know nothing about their friends, and that's just the way this dynamic kind of sets up and works. And again, I don't have anything in common with their classmates' parents by and large, unless I happen to get lucky, and just by chance I happen to find one parent—and that's typically what it is, the *one* parent. Again, by and large, one of the kids will become best friends with that parent's kids because I'm friends with their parents.

With the homeschool group, I'm just amazed because there's the same number—probably like forty-five or fifty families—that I probably get exposed to in a year and a half, families that I hang out with on a regular basis, and [my kids] hang out with their kids on a regular basis. ... The thing that's so cool about it is it doesn't feel like they're hauling me along to go to the party or that I'm hauling them along. They get to see me being friends with grown-up people, and they get to be friends with the kids. Growing up, I didn't know my dad's friends or my mom's friends or what they talked about or how they interacted.

I don't think [homeschooling] affects the time they spend with their friends. I think it affects the amount of time that *we* get to spend together. [Otherwise] they would be spending all that time with their friends, and I would be spending all that time with my friends. We'd just be doing it separate places, and we wouldn't be doing it together. So it doesn't affect the amount of time they spend with their friends. It doesn't affect the amount of TIME that I spend with my friends. It greatly impacts the amount of time that we can spend together, which we never did when they were in school.

[My wife] and I went off to dinner with our friends, and the kids went out with us. [Now] I don't think, "I should be spending this time hanging out with [my kids]." Of course, I'm with them so much anyway that it doesn't matter. ... I don't know that it really comes up with me very often—I probably spend more time with them in a week than a lot of parents do in a month, so I don't really feel a lot of guilt about leaving them to go hang out with [a friend] for a night. So I just don't get that. But again it is nice because I *can* hang out with my friends, and [the kids] can be running around playing and having a good time. I don't feel like I'm taking time away from them. I'm not saying, "Okay guys, see you later. I'm gonna go do an interview." I just think it makes it easier. More natural, less forced.—James, father of three, Durham, NC

Since homeschooling children and parents often spend their days together, sharing educational and other experiences, they get to know and continue to know each other and about each other's lives. In many cases, perhaps due to this, homeschooled kids, including teenagers, often tend to maintain positive, receptive feelings toward their parents.

Home with your family is a safe place, generally—at least it certainly is with us. You might feel more free to discuss things in a more free way than you ever could in a group, ever. I mean, that's the purpose of a family—to have comfort, I guess. It's a better place for being yourself, your real, true, own self.

[I have definitely noticed changes in our family life since I took her out of school.] First of all, there's no stress over homework. That was a really stressful thing for us. When she got home she was exhausted and was supposed to do this homework. She hated the homework, and it was just awful. So that is completely gone from our lives. And now she has homework, but I just say,

"Do you have homework?" and she'll just say, "Yes," or, "No." If she has homework I'll just say, "Well are you going to do it?" and she never says no because she's basically choosing her homework now, so that's definitely different. And if I think about and compare my own relationship with my mom when I was this age with ours, we're closer than my mom and I were, and that shows. She talks to me about stuff, she feels comfortable talking to me about things I wouldn't have felt comfortable talking to my mom about.

Mostly we don't have to fight *about* school, and I don't have to deal with the teachers.
—*Christine, homeschooling mother of one, Durham, NC*

Conflict Resolution Skills

I have seen it happen time and time again: being together in a homeschool environment with their children forces *parents* to learn conflict resolution skills to use in dealing with everyday life. As the parents learn these skills and use them with their children, the children learn them, too.

We have grown into a society in which even our most educated citizens—men and women who can design cities, program computers to do amazing and complicated things, analyze the obscurest poetry—do not feel qualified to raise and educate their own children and often find themselves unable to maintain marriages and healthy family relationships. We send our children off to others' care at younger and younger ages because we feel unprepared to deal with or enjoy spending so much time with them. Perhaps it is time we placed a higher value on the skills required to do what is arguably the most important job available to human beings. Then we could learn those skills and teach them to our children.

Perhaps the greatest gift of homeschooling is a social one: that the choice to homeschool "forces" families to learn how to live together peacefully, how to maintain true discipline and relationships in the household (rather than just the ability to get by and periodically escape), and how to get along and enjoy each other's company (rather than just surviving the finite periods of time between school and sleep).

It is interesting to observe that older homeschooled kids are often fabulous babysitters and often love spending time with younger kids and babies. Why? Because they are raised full time in a family context. They see their younger siblings raised and help with it, they see other homeschoolers' babies and young kids raised, and they see their parents doing the work of raising them.

Freedom to Make Mistakes

One question on the minds of some is, "How can homeschoolers have chances to make mistakes and learn to deal with peer pressure if they are supervised by parents so much?"

The media, for example, talk from both sides of this issue. On the one hand, peer pressure is considered a major cause of problems plaguing children and teenagers in particular; on the other hand, it is considered a necessary part of growing up by opponents of homeschooling. Consider the questions, "Why would one want peer pressure at a young age? Where is any evidence that it is beneficial?"

Sandy, a homeschooling mother of two, responds to the argument that kids need opportunities to "mess up" by being on their own in a school environment, saying:

> One could also argue that kids need to develop strong senses of themselves before they

can learn to handle temptations and their consequences and that those of us who didn't get that opportunity are lucky to have made it this far alive.—*Sandy, mother of two, Chatham County, NC*

Many homeschoolers believe that a safer and more effective method of teaching many life lessons is responsible parental modeling. Homeschooled children, who live lives "off the beaten path," observe first-hand modeling by their parents that it is okay—perhaps even important—to do what you believe is right, regardless of whether the choice is popular.

In fact, homeschooled children themselves grow up with the experience of living "against the grain," amid jeers from some, and get much practice "defending themselves" with the support of parents and other homeschoolers (a lesson that presumably school kids are supposed to learn through dealing with peer pressure). In many cases they are not blindly defending themselves but are standing up proudly for a life they love and believe in. This in and of itself is a daily lesson in coping with and standing up to peer pressure, one that homeschoolers can and do take advantage of.

In fact, the proximity to their parents that homeschooled children enjoy enables them to develop more advanced social skills than would be available to them in just a peer group. Ironically, they may actually have *more* freedom to make mistakes and learn because they are in a safer environment, one where they can receive help and guidance in picking up the pieces.

Three homeschooling mothers share their outlook:

I think interaction with adults is more important [than with peers]. Kids are all learning how to interact. [If you leave kids on their own to socialize each other], you're gonna get mayhem.

That's where the kids learn to pick on each other, whereas if you have adult interaction with it, then you're going to learn how to interact with people appropriately, and you're going to be able to transfer that to interaction with kids. I think about kids who play in like mayhem. That's not the best way to get socialization; that's not the best way to learn to interact with people. The best way they're going to learn to interact with people is with adults or being instructed closely, versus this mass thirty kids in a classroom, sit-in-your-chair-and-don't-talk [approach]. I don't think you're going to learn how to interact with kids and contribute to society in a good way in that environment.

I think [socialization is] an advantage of homeschooling because there's more parental involvement and a better ratio of kid to parent—or child to adult—than there is in a school. There are plenty of opportunities to socialize, which you can keep an eye on, versus just the mayhem of school. You can choose to be there to help them socialize. There are park days and field trips, whereas the school often keeps you out of it. With homeschool you can be involved. If [my son] has a problem during the day interacting with another kid, I can be there to help figure out what the problem was, help him understand why it was a problem, and help him figure out how to handle it differently. I think your parent's involvement in your life is probably the most important involvement in your life, especially when you're young. And so I guess if I was hovering over him and not giving him any space to breathe, then yeah, [he could be stifled], but that's not what it's all about. We give him plenty of space, but then you also are supervising, you're available. While I'm being nearby and available, I'm either visiting with friends, reading a book, doing a craft, taking a walk, or visiting with a friend, so I can be there and be available if I'm needed but not be involved in every conversation.

I think it's a happy medium finding out what that balance is and how to fit but not be on top of them, learning where to pick your fights and learning where to be involved and not be involved. ... So if you're overprotective, then you can stifle them, but that's true of anybody whether you're homeschooling or not. Anybody can stifle. It doesn't mean if you're homeschooling that it's not going to be a problem, but for me it's not, because I'm not an overprotective parent.—*Missy, homeschooling mother of two, Cary, NC*

We've never looked down on them; we value them, and they know that. They do have freedom, and I've also learned to say, "No." We give them freedom, but we also have to be parents. I think a lot of times kids are pushed off into a corner, and they don't see what you go through. Like why you may be tired or sad or something. We let them in on our lives, and they understand that.

They have seen a *lot* of what adults do in the real world. My son's an athlete and a triathlete, my daughter has been to NOCIRC [National Organization of Circumcision Information Resource Centers] conferences and midwifery conferences, when I'm not around they can make dinner, and if a car battery dies, they can jumpstart a battery. My son's friends say that he makes the best broccoli, they like his broccoli, and they don't even know how to make broccoli. [These are] things you do that you just take for granted. We almost don't notice the things they can do until we meet someone who can't do it.—*Laurie, homeschooling mother of two, Katonah, NY*

We all want our children to be able to face life challenges, peer pressure, and all the evils of the world with strength and integrity. They have a much better shot at this if they have the time and support to develop and grow first. Children cannot make wise choices until they have the perspective and information about themselves and what's in front of them. When they are young, they are mostly influenced by their environment. It takes time for them to be able to understand an issue to be able to make judgments about it and act in their own best interest and in the interest of others.

At each age there are things they can handle with wisdom and things they cannot. Our public schools inundate children with things they are not equipped to handle. I want my children to experience age-appropriate amounts of challenge and difficult choice-making. I want to help them think it through. I want to control, to some extent, the amount of exposure they face to the challenges of peer-dominated cultural influences, because I believe that our country is assuming that children should be rushed to grow up, and it is hurting them. They are toughening up to it but at a personal cost. And that will cost us all.—*Janice, homeschooling mother of two, Durham, NC*

Siblings

"We have flown the air like birds and swum the sea like fishes, but have yet to learn the simple act of walking the earth like brothers."
—*Dr. Martin Luther King, Jr.*

One commonly acknowledged benefit of homeschooling is that it somehow encourages closer sibling relationships. One has only to observe a few homeschooling families to know that this is so. Lee

Stewart observes that her children, since becoming homeschoolers, have become better friends with each other and their parents, don't argue as much, and work and play better together. She notes that this also is reflected in their relationships and dealings with others (Stewart 1990). David Guterson observes that "homeschooled siblings must live and learn with one another, and the intensity and meaning of their relationship, its daily depth and fragility, become the standard for future relationships" (Guterson 1992).

The relationships children have with their siblings are sometimes made light of, but they are no insignificant thing. If indeed these act as the standard for future relationships, then we would certainly all want our children to learn skills and standards for dealing with one another in respectful and effective ways. There is no doubt that homeschooled children know each other better, spend more time together, and are required, through living together full time (rather than "escaping" to school each day), to learn skills and also standards for dealing with one another in respectful and effective ways:

> I encourage them to be friends with each other, as I feel that will be most important as they are adults. That was another reason I decided to homeschool: I noticed that my oldest stopped getting along with her little sister when she went to school.—*Sue, homeschooling mother of three, upstate New York*

Moreover, the relationships we develop with our parents and siblings do not become a thing of the past when we reach adulthood, but remain with us, supporting us and enriching and bringing meaning to our lives. Our relationships with our parents and siblings, good or bad, are there for us throughout the rest of our lives, particularly if we are given the chance and help needed to develop positive, loving ones while we are young.

"Problem Child" or "Gifted Child"

Homeschooling and learning in a family context may be particularly meaningful in the case of "problem" or "gifted" children. Ironically, the "problem" child and the "gifted" child are often one and the same. If labels ("problem," "gifted," "hyperactive," and the list goes on) were removed, many of these children could otherwise be described as bored, different, intelligent, creative, underappreciated, unsuited to the classroom environment, energetic, misunderstood, spirited, and so forth. Being labeled in negative ways can affect a child's self-esteem and social health forever. For this reason, these "different" children especially benefit from being in a more individualized environment with a caring individual who is genuinely interested and invested in his well-being and who is truly motivated and has good reason to appreciate his individuality. (Of course, the child cannot expect such special attention in adulthood, but as a child she benefits from it and can learn skills that will enable her to be a successful adult.) Such a person can be motivated to spend time, get to know the child, and come to recognize her challenges as the gifts they are so the child may learn to use the gifts behind each challenge in a positive manner. When a parent can take the time to discover and understand these gifts, he has done the child a priceless service that will fortify him for the rest of his life. In many cases, a parent is equipped to provide this service in a way that no one else can.

Often, "problem" behaviors disappear just by removing the child from school. This is undoubtedly partly due to the sudden reduction in ratio. Moreover, many parents have related that their children, viewed as problem children in school, show themselves to be extremely creative, persistent, intelligent, and passionate when removed from the unnaturally restrictive and conformity-oriented setting of school. These parents see it as part of their jobs (as parents and home educators) to help their children learn to channel these two-sided traits positively. In school, such qualities and behaviors, which may not fit in well to the routine and one-size-fits-all structure of school, are often simply discouraged and even punished.

A Word About Spirituality

We must remember that intelligence is not enough. Intelligence plus character—that is the goal of true education. The complete education gives one not only power of concentration, but worthy objectives upon which to concentrate.—Dr. Martin Luther King, Jr.

One of the most widespread illusions about homeschooling is that it is done primarily for religious reasons. This is not so; though many families do homeschool with religious reasons in mind, it is a far smaller percentage than most imagine (33 percent of homeschoolers, in 2000, according to the US Census Bureau). And those who do cite religious reasons also cite other reasons as well, such as believing their children can get a better academic education at home (Bauman 2001).

In fact, there really isn't a clear division between homeschool families who homeschool for religious reasons and those who do so for academic or other reasons. The division is imaginary because the vast majority of so-called religious homeschoolers do so for religious, academic, and social reasons, and so-called secular homeschoolers do so for not only academic and social but also spiritual reasons. These spiritual reasons can include traditional religious agendas, such as teaching Christian, Jewish, Muslim, Native American, or other values and traditions, or other spiritual beliefs and values not strictly associated with organized religion, such as being a good person; living in harmony with nature, God, or the universe; practicing meditation; Bible study; and so on.

Spirituality, even for atheists and agnostics, is a part of life and family and therefore a part of every family's homeschooling experience. Since homeschooling is a way of life, every aspect of life is part of the learning process.

In general, families have found that homeschooling, largely because of the family unity it encourages, nourishes a healthy spiritual life whether a family practices formal or theistic religion or not. One father shares his view:

> We have experienced lots of spiritual benefits from homeschooling. Just the fact that he's with us or a member of [our religious] community, and we share basic spiritual values that come up all the time on a day-to-day basis. I think part of the problem is that in public school you can't mention God, and in a lot of the parochial schools you can't mention anything but God—and a very specific god. I certainly support church-going, but I think most spiritual work is done in the day-to-day, in opportunities that come up, and through questions that arise that you wouldn't really foresee.
>
> I think a lot of the benefit of homeschooling is just that you spend more time with the child. Period. And no matter what goes on, he's going to

get a better sense of what his parents' values are, and I think that's unbelievably important. It's a relatively recent phenomenon to send your kids off to a "factory" to get educated, and I wasn't really aware of that until we got into homeschooling. That whole socialization thing is the big fear; *I* counter that spending twelve years only with kids your own age and one or two grownups—*that's* pretty strange. I mean what does *that* teach you? No grandparents, no older kids, no younger kids.

A lot of [the benefit of homeschooling] is just time spent together and teaching him our values and sharing our perspective and being there to answer his questions.—*Steven, homeschooling father of one, Mebane, NC*

Family Time vs. the Cycle of Detachment

Experts recognize, and most people would probably agree, that time with family is crucial to children's development. Children are socialized first and foremost at home in the context of the family. The family life is most likely the primary factor and predictor of current and future happiness, social success, and so on. Homeschooling families don't have to try to cram their "quality time" into short, pre-scheduled intervals, such as dinnertime, Saturdays, or the annual week-long family vacation. Instead, they are free to stop and enjoy the quality (and quantity) time as it occurs naturally, just as many do with their other learning experiences.

In their book, *What's A Smart Woman Like You Doing At Home?*, Linda Burton, Janet Dittmer, and Cheri Loveless point out, "As much as we would like to deny it, women are in truth discovering that children rarely need their mothers at their mothers' convenience" (Burton, et al 1986). This applies to their need for both parents and for family time in general. Even though homeschoolers spend plenty of time with friends and away from parents, still the time with family usually far outweighs the time they would have together without homeschooling. Homeschooling allows parents and children to have both quality *and* quantity time, while also having plenty of social time with non-family-members. This results in less pressure to really get a lot from the quality time regardless of moods, circumstances, and other factors.

In his books, child expert Dr. William Sears refers to what he calls "the detachment snowball." According to this idea, the more time parents and kids spend apart, the less parents know and understand their kids; the less responsive, respectful, and communicative both parents and kids become; and the more time both need away from each other (Sears 1993). Dr. Sears no doubt had babies and very young children in mind, but this phenomenon nevertheless applies throughout childhood.

David Guterson similarly points out that parents often comment on the negative ways school has affected their children: "It is part of the growing alienation they feel from their children, who gradually become estranged from them as they become ever more deeply immersed in the universe of their school peers—an alienation parents erroneously conclude is a "natural" part of their children's growing up, a necessary prerequisite to their independent adulthood. This distance, though, is far from natural, and the dismay parents feel about it ought not to be repressed" (Guterson 1992).

Conversely, homeschooling parents and kids often grow to know each other better and better as time goes on, and the benefits are obvious to those who have experienced them:

> Having been on both sides (having your children in school vs. homeschooling), I have come to a realization. When they are in school, you become somewhat disconnected from them. When you are not working with them every day you lose sight of their accomplishments, you may not be aware of what they are capable of, and you may not readily see how they are growing and who they are becoming as they evolve into their own unique person. I think when they are in school, there is also less time to fit in extracurricular activities, so the over-scheduling syndrome occurs; the kids have little time to just play and be imaginative.
>
> My observations about homeschool families [are as follows]: they tend to be more relaxed, the kids seem to be more inclined to participate in imaginative play when they get together, they are more inclusive, and they listen to each other and show respect towards each other. Homeschool parents seem to listen to their kids and view them as more capable. The parent-child interactions seem more equal in that it is okay to have a give-and-take with your child without being viewed as the child manipulating the parent. Maybe this is because there is a better understanding of the child by the parent.
>
> I also think homeschool kids are more comfortable interacting with adults and sharing what they have learned or telling an adult what they think with the expectation that the adult will be interested and want to hear what they have to say. I find adults who do not homeschool are not quite sure how to react to this; some rise to the opportunity to have an interesting discussion with a child, others brush them aside, unwilling to give

credit where it is due because it is a child who is engaging them in an intellectual discussion.
—*Molly, homeschooling mother of two, West Grove, PA*

Moreover, through devoting their time to being with and learning to be with their kids, parents have the opportunity to gain skill and confidence in their abilities as parents:

For my husband and I, homeschooling just seemed to be a natural extension of the "attachment parenting" of our babies and toddlers. We had spent the early years excitedly, eagerly learning alongside our children, and we couldn't imagine sending them away for a huge chunk of the day when they reached "school age." We wanted to continue on the journey of discovery that we began together, not put them on a new boat to sail alone without us.

Today I think we would say that our relationships with our children are most important. Some people choose to homeschool because they feel that their children will get a better quality education at home. I agree that happens, but I think that is a side effect of the good relationships we have with our children. I think that building that relationship is the foundation for all other relationships, activities, learning, and work in their lives. And I don't think I could have as close a relationship with my children if I sent them away to public schools. Then I would merely be a spectator of a major portion of their life. Of course I want my children to be educated enough to sustain themselves in adult society, to develop a love of reading and learning, and to discover the vocation in which they are most gifted. But I believe all of those things will naturally grow up when we focus on our relationship with our children and strive to really know them. There is no other person in the world who knows our children as well, or loves them as much as my husband and me. Who better then to "teach" them or, as we see it, to learn alongside them and prepare them for life? And what better way is there to learn about life than to live it alongside someone you love?

On a personal level, I think family unity is important to help our children understand how to have relationships with other people—to have the skills necessary to interact with others in all kinds of situations. If children don't have strong, loving relationships with their parents, it becomes difficult to form healthy relationships with other people—and that can be a life-long challenge. No one knows our own children better than we do, and there is no one our children trust as much as their own parents (when the relationships are healthy). Even the very best public school teacher will never have the same knowledge of my child as I do—and she will never be able to specifically meet the individual needs of my child the way I will. You cannot spend a significant portion of your day separated from your child and expect that your relationship will be unaffected.

On a larger level, I believe the decay of family unity is at the heart of many of the social problems our culture is facing today. Our culture is in a hurry to rush little four- and five-year-olds off to public school, where they are placed in a room full of ten to twenty other little children with only one or two teachers. Then parents are shocked and horrified when these same children, years later, have become completely peer dependent and cannot identify with their own family. But peer dependence is the natural outcome of public education because a child has a real and intense need for relationship. When that need for relationship cannot be met by an adult (a teacher who is working with many students), then the child will turn to the only other available person, the peer in the classroom. Consequently, a child comes to value the opinions of his school-age peers more than those of his family because his relationships with his peers are stronger than his relationship with his parents. Our children are starving for meaningful relationships and will engage in all kinds of unhealthy activities and behaviors to fulfill that innate need for intimacy. What a tragedy that we have divided the family for the sake of "education." Strong family relationships and unity are at the heart of healthy communities—the latter cannot exist in the absence of the former.—*Amy, homeschooling mother of three, upstate New York*

The strong family relationships and quantity time with parents that homeschoolers enjoy end up being a great boon to children socially (as well as in other ways).

But...?

Don't they need to actually get in *trouble* to learn to handle peer pressure, temptations, and consequences? And don't they need to encounter bullies? These concerns are commonly expressed in many forms. In the next chapter, we will fully address these concerns and explore the question of whether and to what extent kids need to experience adversity and encounter bullies to develop social strength and decision-making skills.

chapter six

SAFETY, ADVERSITY, AND BULLYING

"Without complete parental control, [children] are forced to grow up too quickly and miss certain aspects of development. Knowing that you can depend on others and you deserve their support is a strong foundation for eventually developing independence and autonomy."—John Gray, Ph.D., Children Are From Heaven

"If there were no other reason for wanting to keep kids out of school, the social life would be reason enough."—John Holt, Teach Your Own

Adversity is something that all human beings must deal with in some form during both childhood and adulthood. Becoming prepared for it may well be an important task of childhood. How, one might reasonably ask, can kids experience adversity and learn to deal with it if their parents are around so much of the time?

One answer is that life is full of "opportunities" to experience adversity, with parents nearby or not, and homeschoolers, who can easily seek guidance from their parents, may be in a unique position to learn to cope with it in a positive way when it happens.

It would be easy to assume that kids need to be on their own to learn to deal with difficult situations, such as bullying, peer pressure, and so on, since they will be on their own in the future when such situations arise. On the other hand, the same logic could be used to say that children don't need parents at all—that they should be completely on their own, since they won't always have parents to take care of them. Such a claim would of course be ridiculous; although it is true that children won't always have parents to take care of them, we recognize that *now,* while they are very young and still very vulnerable, they need our protection and thus need to live in the safety of a family. (Indeed, this is why families and parents exist.) When they grow up and move on, they will certainly face dangers and challenges, but as adults they will be capable and prepared to handle these. They will have become prepared by having grown up close to and observing adults make wise choices and handle problems. They will also become prepared by gradually taking on more freedom and responsibility as they are ready.

It may seem useful in theory for kids to have a chance to experience things away from their parents, but in specific, some questions must be asked about this. What are these things kids "need" to experience (that their parents theoretically wouldn't let them do), and why would we want them to experience such things if they are things parents wouldn't want them to do? If it is adverse experiences we feel they need, why should they, as children, have to experience these things without their parents on hand for guidance and help? Or why should they experience things that can only be experienced away from parents? If asked, how many parents (of school-going kids or otherwise) would really want their kids to be out experiencing drugs, sex, fights, or other such things that require non-supervision in order to take place?

There is a reason that most parents have a protective feeling toward their kids: they are programmed to, because as far as nature is concerned, it is their job. Children can and do learn to deal with dangers and pressures by observing how their parents deal with these things and by dealing with them themselves using the guidance, if they choose to seek it, of their parents. When a parent protects a child from a dangerous or unhealthy situation, the child observes that his or her safety and well-being are important to the parent, and on some level the child internalizes and learns from this reaction. He may also learn how to avoid such circumstances by watching his parents' modeling and listening to his parents' guidance as to what to do. In fact, when being protected or advocated for by the parent, a child may be in a particularly receptive position to be open to parental teaching or advice.

Physical Safety

We chose homeschooling because we didn't like some of the things [my daughter] learned in school and on the bus. Also because of her (and the other girls [have it], too) dairy allergy it was difficult, especially at birthdays and holidays. One incident also convinced us: One day shortly before we moved, in a small-town K-12 school, it was a 70F+ day, and she came home and told us they weren't allowed to go out at recess. [We] found out it was because a teenager was outside the school threatening a teacher.

I felt that I could keep her safer at home or wherever I went than sending her to school where there were so many unknowns. The principal decided that for the safety of the kids they would keep them inside that day. That was probably a good idea, but it just made me realize that the kids weren't as safe as with me, or at least I would be aware of the danger immediately.—Sue, homeschooling mother of three, upstate New York

Bullies

Relatives and friends of homeschoolers commonly express concern that homeschooled children will not have to learn to deal with bullies. This concern is common, even though parents of schoolchildren generally do not want their children to encounter bullies. This concern is in some ways a paradox. On the one hand, the concerned individuals are right: bullying is not a major problem in the homeschooling community as it is in schools. Most homeschoolers consider this an advantage, not a drawback, of homeschooling. (School experts, too, have begun to regard bullying as a problem, not as the positive socialization experience or necessary evil that some parents and school personnel have viewed it to be, a fact that will be discussed later in this chapter.) On the other hand, bullying can sometimes occur in homeschooling communities, even if to a lesser degree than in schools (for example, leaving other children out, name-calling, and so on). When this happens, the children have a perfect opportunity not just to *encounter* bullying, but to learn skills to deal with it due to one key reason: *their parents are there to help them.* Homeschooled children, who tend to have good relationships with their parents, will often go to their parents and ask for assistance with difficult interpersonal or other situations and thus can learn to resolve or avoid them safely. This does not mean that the parents are sheltering the child or solving the problem for them; rather, the parents are protecting their child while teaching (or modeling) skills for future or current use.

Bullying is a problem

Despite some individuals' concerns that homeschooled children are "missing out" on exposure to bullies, school personnel and other experts now consider bullying to be a significant problem for children. The National School Safety Center says that bullying is a major problem in American schools (www.nssc1.org). Whereas bullying used to be considered just child's play to be tolerated or ignored, now it has escalated to a point where school children are in serious danger from bullying. Now it may involve guns, and children may miss school or become afraid to go to the bathroom. It has been found to cause lower academic performance, increased absence from school, and, of course, social stigma for the victim (Smith-Heavenrich 2001). Bullying is a real problem, and protection from that problem is just another advantage of homeschooling. (A list of Web sites with information about the issue of bullying can be found in Appendix A under "Helpful Web sites.")

Bullying is less common
among homeschoolers

Homeschooling essentially eliminates the bullying problem because it just doesn't seem to happen much in the homeschool community. Why? There are several possible reasons. For one thing, homeschoolers tend to receive lots of parental attention and guidance and are therefore less likely to bully. In an article titled, "What Causes Bullies?" Jane St. Clair reports that bullies often come from families in which the parents are overly permissive, "discipline inconsistently," or "do not monitor his activities or take an interest in his life" (St. Clair 2006). Furthermore, the presence of parents nearby may also result in a lessened likelihood of their children being the victims of bullying. Young kids supervised by parents aren't as likely to have to fend for themselves before they are ready. Although some minor forms of bullying can occur, such as name-calling, excluding, and so forth, I have never heard of a case in which a child was "beaten up" or otherwise seriously victimized by another homeschooled child. I suspect any such occurrence is extremely rare.

Of course, bullying and other dangerous encounters can occur with strangers outside the homeschool community, and, as with many other aspects of their education, homeschoolers are attentive to preparing their kids for the future. Many homeschooling parents provide their kids with a variety of forms of preparation for adverse situations, including enrolling them in martial arts classes, spending time teaching and practicing conflict resolution skills, and so on.

Homeschoolers believe their children are best prepared for the future by being protected as well as educated to deal with future situations in a safe environment. I have never heard anyone suggest that babies need to be left alone with open fires so they could learn to deal with fire; this would be inappropriate because fire is dangerous, and the baby, who is too young to protect herself from that situation, would get hurt. Still, supervising small children around fire does not mean that they will never learn to avoid fire or how to put one out. Likewise, supervising children as they learn to deal with adverse situations does not mean they will not know how to protect themselves as they grow and gain greater independence. Many homeschoolers count the absence of significant danger from bullying as a very positive trait of homeschooling:

> My children have all been harmed physically and emotionally by the [public school] system. The most extreme: My youngest was knocked out in the boys' room in second grade and still has residual problems. One of the things I noticed almost immediately is that our relationships improved dramatically after returning to homeschooling. I think the stress and exhaustion we were all feeling obliterated any ability to relate in a calm and loving way. After coming home and being able to go at a sane pace, we all relaxed and had energy to relate in more positive ways.
>
> The differences in the social experiences are profound. Everything from being physically harmed to being teased and shamed [has turned around]. [My son] was knocked out in the boy's room in second grade and has problems to this day as a result; he was beaten up on a regular basis as well. [My daughter] was knocked around because she was very small for her age and sometimes not noticed as kids raced through the halls passing from class to class. When we socialize with the homeschoolers in our groups, the children have a lot more fun, and "politics" and disagreements are a rarity. I have waited in the office reading, while my son is in his class at school, and I am amazed at the way children are spoken to by those "in authority." Not all, but most people talk down to kids and often use a tone of voice that implies shame and disrespect. It upsets me to hear this, and when you multiply that by six hours by 180 days, no wonder our kids are hurting in this society.
>
> Benefits my children receive by being home educated: a calmer and more relaxed family life, a safer and more enjoyable social life, the freedom

to explore their own interests, time to think, experiences and relationships with other aspects of society that they wouldn't be able to have if in school (my son earned $130 selling cold drinks to the paving crews in our neighborhood), freedom to travel whenever we want, being able to go as deep into a subject as they want, not having to submit to disparaging and disrespectful authority figures, avoiding pointless homework, studying in an atmosphere of comfort (physically and emotionally), and avoiding negative peer influences. There are probably others, but that's all I can think of right now. If I had had my way, my children would have NEVER gone to public school. However, we have dealt with what life handed us, and I know my kids will be okay in the long run.—*Lauriann, mother of three, Las Vegas, NV*

Parents often comment that the reduced stress from not having to worry about bullies and other social and physical safety issues reflects very clearly on their family relationships:

We have homeschooled since our children were born in 1991 and 1995. There was never a conscious decision to homeschool; it evolved over time. When my oldest son was born, I [met] a woman who homeschooled her children (teens at the time). I asked her why, and she told me that she "wanted to raise her own children." That always stayed in my mind. I really didn't like some of the nasty behaviors I was seeing in the media and on our own street and didn't want my kids behaving like that, too. Through her, I met other families that homeschool, and gradually, we just began. Now my kids really don't want to go to school. I think they like the laid-back attitude we have at home.

Benefits for them, that's harder to categorize. They are not exposed to as much bullying. The local high schools hire off-duty police to patrol their dances. We have Brampton's gangs peddling drugs, violence, [and so forth]. I know our police force is busy at the schools for many incidents. [My oldest son] (twelve) is very shy, more so with his peers. He finds it very hard to fit it, but over time, finds his niche. He might be an easy target for bullies. He is in our local Scout troop and certainly shows no sign of shyness there; he can be as obnoxious as any of the Scouts.

The most important benefit I can see is the relationship we have together. We are very close. I believe I can stick my neck out and say that we are friends, too, not just parent and child. I wouldn't trade this time with them for anything. We have little cash, but we have a wonderful relationship. I like that the boys are so close to us. For me, it means that they have someone they can always trust, to listen and be there, someone they can always come to for whatever reason. I want our kids to feel close to us and each other. Family is important.—*Susan, homeschooling mother of two, Orangeville, Ontario*

Social Safety

Many homeschoolers believe that during childhood, children need to engage in social learning, too, within the safety of a family and with the guidance of parents who love and care for them and have their best interests at heart. Later in life, they will experience the same social challenges everyone does on their own, but they will be older and better equipped to handle these challenges at that time.

To put it another way, social health can be likened to physical health. A healthy social life is like good nutrition. Better food, not just more food, is needed to promote optimum health. A certain quantity is needed, of course, but the quality of the food is just as, if not more so, important to one's well-being. Even though our children will have to make their own healthy food choices later in life, or perhaps *because* they will have to, we feed them as healthy a diet as we can. Few would suggest that children need to be fed unhealthy foods in childhood because they will be exposed to unhealthy food options later in life. It just wouldn't make sense. Instead, we try to feed them nutritious foods so they will grow up healthy and strong, and their bodies will be more resilient and able to cope with whatever they encounter later on, be it illness, an absence of nutritious food options, or whatever else. By feeding our children healthy foods, we also teach them that we believe good nutrition is important, and they come to think of whatever we usually feed them as the norm. Later, they will be exposed to (and doubtless consume) less nutritious foods, but ultimately, they may remember and return to the healthier diet on which they were raised.

Similarly, the argument that kids need to be away from their parents and experience adversity because it is more "realistic" sounds logical, but in fact is not when looked at more closely. We do not let newborn babies ride in cars without car seats just because they will not use car seats as adults; we want them to be safe now while they are more vulnerable. When they are older and ready, we will take them out and put them in a seatbelt. We hope that as adults, they will remember that we made them wear a seatbelt and will continue to wear one, rather than never having learned to. The fact that we are there, time and time again, reminding them to wear their seatbelts makes them safer now and prepares them with habits that will keep them safe during adulthood as well. (Had they ridden alone in the car with no guidance but other young children, who themselves would not know to wear their seatbelts, they would never develop this habit. Even though they will ride without their parents in later life, riding without them as a young child would do nothing to prepare them for adulthood.)

The same can be applied to social skills: Having a parent on hand for guidance with social interactions actually fortifies a child with skills and habits that will help her deal with future social situations more skillfully and readily.

If charged with the responsibility of training a child to become a tight-rope walker, we would not expect them to get up on the rope early on with no net simply because this is more like the "real show." We would perhaps start them off on a low, wide balance beam, holding their hand while they figure out how to walk on it. Gradually we would try them on a narrower beam, and a higher one, until they were able to practice walking the rope. Even after all this preliminary training, we would provide them with a net because we care about their safety. Only when they had mastered the tight rope and were fully trained and confident in their ability to proceed safely would we remove the net. This would not be considered overprotective, and the presence of the net or the supervision would in no way interfere with the learning process.

We don't need to go out of our way to expose our kids to social adversity or negative social settings. They will encounter adversity later in life, and by raising them in a socially "safe" environment, preparing them with modeling, guidance, values, and love, they will have the resilience to handle whatever situations may arise later on. They will grow and move on, and they will remember that we consider family and values important—they have their whole childhoods behind them to prove it. Ideally, they will consider this the norm: valuing family, being protected by (and protecting) the ones they love, and feeling secure, rather than being alone in a dog-eat-dog social environment. People live out their expectations of themselves and of life. If a child grows up expecting a positive social experience, he will create it around him for his entire life.

Well-known psychologist and author John Gray, in his book *Children Are From Heaven,* states that young children cannot be expected to make decisions and, if required to, will miss out on an important aspect of their childhood (Gray 1999). There is plenty of time in life for them to make decisions. First they must watch their parents model years and years of good decision-making, and they must observe their parents making the careful decisions that they believe are in the child's (and whole family's) best interests. In this way the child can learn firstly, that he is worthy of taking care of and should thus take care of himself, and secondly, that just as his parents make decisions with the whole family's best interests in mind, so, too, can and should he make decisions that take into account both his best interests and the best interests of others. The family is the perfect, naturally-designed situation for learning these things.

> I don't think at five or even six years old a child has enough of a foundation in the values I hope to teach them to go out into a classroom for a stranger to teach them ideas that I may or may not believe in or agree with. However, we don't homeschool for religious reasons. Because we spend so much time together, conflicts have to be worked through and good communication maintained. Every day I am called on to examine my choices as a parent and teacher. I have to work

with my kids to problem solve, to make sure we have a balance in our lives of work and play. I think it would have been "easier" to send my children off to school and let the so-called experts tell me what is best for them, but when I really thought about what happens in school, I saw a system that doesn't allow for difference, that creates a highly artificial environment (age segregation, product over process, erratic curriculum), and I simply thought it was bizarre.

My thinking is that children are not fully aware of right and wrong, actions and consequences at the age our culture typically sends them to school. That is, they can act "right" but don't [have] a firm inner voice or moral compass to keep them on track. I know in the Catholic Church age seven is the age of reason, the time when children are held accountable for their actions. This seems to me to be about the time most kids start to develop that inner guidance. I think Dr. Sears [child expert Dr. William Sears] calls it an inner feeling of rightness, that children learn to identify that inner feeling of rightness and want to maintain that feeling. I know there is no way, by age five, my children had learned and internalized the kind of value system I hope to instill in them, and I was not going to send them out for the majority of their waking hours for a stranger to raise them.—*Sara, homeschooling mother of two, Bowling Green, OH*

Families experience many benefits as a result of the physical, emotional, and social safety that homeschooling has to offer. And with these benefits in place, homeschoolers are free to enjoy another great gift of homeschooling (which we will explore in the next chapter): the time to be a kid.

chapter seven

FREEDOM AND TIME TO BE A KID (BEFORE HAVING TO BE GROWN UP)

"For an institution to ask you, during some of your most magical years, to sit still and be good and read quietly for six or more hours each day, is barely thinkable, let alone tolerable."—Grace Llewellyn,
The Teenage Liberation Handbook

C ritics of homeschooling have occasionally pointed out that kids need a chance to be kids before having to be adults. This is certainly true, and I think it would be difficult to find a homeschooler who disagreed with it. In fact, it seems a somewhat ironic criticism of homeschooling, in light of homeschoolers' real experiences with childhood.

A close look at the lives of real homeschoolers reveals that, in truth, homeschooling allows children the opportunity to truly be kids to a degree that has become rare in this culture.

Paradoxically, school, while being held up as synonymous with childhood itself, may actually deny children the opportunity to really be kids, requiring them instead to sit still, be quiet, and have enormous responsibility in the form of daily work for which they are judged, graded, and tracked for the rest of their childhoods.

People who are stuck in school all day and then have homework—they have no time to be kids. They're always in this structured environment. They don't have time to play with their friends, they have to be quiet at lunch, they have to be quiet during class, they get in trouble for getting up and talking to other kids; it's just too much structure and restraints put on kids when kids just need to be kids. It teaches kids to be robots; ...they're not built to be sitting in a desk all day.

[I think having time to be a kid means having time] to explore things, to find out what their interests are, to have free time around an open area of things to play, to just not be structured and not have structured requirements to turn in at the end. I think natural curiosity and wanting to learn will allow them to explore the areas that they need to for whatever they want to do. And my job is basically to be there to facilitate and give him access to stuff when he has an interest. So I'm not going to have all the answers for things, but if he wants to do electronics or something, then I would be there to help him find the information and get him to the library. If he needs equipment to do that, then we would get him the equipment. I think that whenever kids have a passion, that leads them to explore things more deeply. And they want to; you don't have to make them do it, they want to. And they'll just fly with it.—*Missy, homeschooling mother of two, Cary, NC*

Instead of sitting with hands folded and mouths closed at a desk for the better part of six hours a day, carrying loads of books and responsibilities, waking up every morning to an alarm clock and returning to the stress of the daily school "grind," homeschooled kids are often found doing the very kinds of things that make childhood childhood: frolicking with their friends in the river, reading Dr. Seuss and the Chronicles of Narnia, drawing colorful pictures with crayons, dashing eagerly from favorite exhibit to favorite exhibit in the museum, catching frogs and butterflies, kicking a ball in the yard, baking muffins with chunky measuring cups, writing in their diaries, digging for fossils, playing board games, going to the theater, visiting the zoo, helping assemble new bikes (then riding them), playing the guitar, writing poems, designing magnificent Lego castles, having friends over, climbing in the park, doing their chores, talking to grandparents about the old days, counting change, peddling rocks door-to-door (sliding scale based on amount of change in buyer's pocket at time of purchase), having birthday parties, making angels in the snow, going to storytelling festivals, playing hard, and taking naps. Homeschooling parents want their kids to get an excellent education *and* be happy while they're getting it. And experience says they can have both.

Stephanie, an eighteen-year-old from Katonah, New York, who was homeschooled until college, tells of her experience:

> We really got to spend our time getting into things that were really our interests. And we could choose when and where. On a beautiful day like today (it's seventy degrees and clear and breezy out), I could take my books and go sit out on the trampoline, at a picnic table, or wherever and do my work out there and enjoy the sun. I like not being stuck in a building. I really liked being able to choose where and when I do a subject.

119

She adds:

We did lots of activities; we went to the art center, once a week we did pottery on the wheel, we did origami, went ice skating every Tuesday, went on hikes together, went to plays, movies, wilderness experiences. There were always things going on where the [homeschooling] group would get together, and [our family would] sort of pick and choose.—*Stephanie, eighteen years old, homeschooled until college, Katonah, NY*

Aric, a twelve-year-old from Michigan, says:

[Homeschooling']s more fun. It's just easier, I guess. I get to do stuff when other kids aren't around, like I get to play at the park alone with no kids around because I'm shy. I get to jump on the trampoline more. I get to do a lot of stuff more. I get to play with my toys more and my dog and my cat. I can't think of anything I don't like about it. I guess I could say doing math.—*Aric, homeschooled twelve-year-old, Michigan*

Ann, a homeschooling mother from Chapel Hill, North Carolina, found that her daughter was more able to be a kid when she started homeschooling:

[My daughter] went to school for half a year of kindergarten. And then I took her out. Why? Because she was just wilting on the vine. She would fall asleep at the supper table, literally. Lay her head down on the supper table and fall asleep. We just thought that the day was too long. ... [There were] so many reasons, but we would pick her up in the afternoon, and she would just melt down in the car from meanness that had happened on the playground and I think just the stress of being told what to do all day. She's so much happier now.—*Ann, homeschooling mother of two, Chapel Hill, NC*

And her daughter, Haleigh, shares her own perspective:

[When you go to school] you have to wake up at a crazy time like 6:00, 6:30, or something—sometimes 5:00. ...When I was just starting in kindergarten, I was always tired and fell asleep at the dinner table and stuff. Mom thought it was just because I was getting settled in and ready and I would just get over it, but no, I didn't. And then she said, "Well, how about you go for a couple more months and (just before Christmas) we'll ask your principal and you'll stop." And so I got really excited and I started to perk up a little 'cause I was getting really close, and I kept asking my teacher how many more days until Christmas.

I'm way more awake now and happy. ... I get up whenever, usually at 9, 9:30, and I do a little bit of schoolwork. Then I just do one section of my room—I don't clean up the whole room if it's a mess, I just clean up my bookshelf one day, or I just clean up my desk. Then I have to feed my hamster and play with her, and sometimes I sweep the deck of leaves or something like that. And then we play.—*Haleigh, nine-year-old homeschooler, Chapel Hill, NC*

Some have observed that homeschooled children in general seem to exhibit less "childish" behavior. A 1992 study by Shyers, for example, found that homeschoolers were more patient and less competitive, tended to introduce themselves to one another more, didn't fight as much, and so on (Shyers 1992). This is sometimes interpreted as a sign that these homeschoolers are somehow "missing out" on childhood. This quick interpretation is understandable, because culturally, we have sadly come to equate childhood with fighting, bickering, self-consciousness, rudeness, and a disdain for adults or authority figures.

As a result, kids who demonstrate respect, good manners, and an interest in adult conversations (even as they also play, laugh, and participate in healthy childhood activities) seem out of the ordinary, and even some adults feel uncomfortable with this difference. But what if those behaviors (rudeness, disrespect, lack of interest in "grown-up" matters, and so forth) are not inherent to childhood but are in fact unhealthy behaviors learned in school? Could it be that *exposure* to this kind of negativity, not the absence of it, constitutes missing out on the innocence of childhood? It is well known that very young children love to—and need to—imitate adults in order to learn and develop. When not taught to mistrust or shun adults, kids will often continue this kind of interest in and imitation of adults, and it can be argued that this, indeed, is a natural and healthy aspect of childhood. Homeschooled children are sometimes frowned upon by others for listening to and participating in adults' conversations (they don't know their "place," the argument goes). But from another perspective, they, like all children, simply have a natural curiosity and interest in all things around them, but, unlike many children, they have not grown to view adults as "the enemy" or learning itself as something boring to be shunned.

"Missing Out" on School Life

Similarly, critics of homeschooling sometimes comment that homeschoolers miss out on certain cultural "rites of passage" or "rites of childhood" that we, a culture full of people who went to school, have come to think of as important childhood experiences— for example, riding the bus, attending the prom, going to football games, and so on. Perhaps, though, these things are not inherent or important rites of *childhood*, but are in fact only rites of *school-going*. Here again, we may be influenced by our tendency to equate school with childhood. But in actuality, a childhood in school is only one kind of childhood—a relatively new one, in fact. Throughout most of history, and in most cultures, childhood has not included school or any of the trappings we now associate with it. It is possible that the childhood of the future will not include it, either.

But, one could argue, nevertheless they are the rites of childhood in this, a predominantly school-going culture. Indeed, they may well be experiences that most children today do go through. But does that make them good?

Interestingly, homeschooled children, who are frequently questioned and are often well aware of the school rituals they are not participating in, do not necessarily feel that they are "missing out."

Francis, a thirteen-year-old homeschooler from Boynton Beach, Florida, says this:

> "The social aspects [of homeschooling] are probably not the same way they would be in school, [but] I'm not saying it's worse. I've missed out on something; I wouldn't say [what I've missed out on] is good, though."—*Francis, thirteen-year-old homeschooler, Boynton Beach, FL*

When Sebastien, a twelve-year-old public schooler from a large city, who had been homeschooled for three years, was asked whether he felt he had missed out on anything by homeschooling, he had this to say (names and some identifying details in the following account have been changed):

> "Not really. I liked homeschooling a lot. I can't say anything bad about it. Now, [in school], I miss things. I miss being able to say that I want to learn about something and learning about it."
> —*Sebastien, twelve-year-old, previously homeschooled*

And Zach, a homeschooling father from Hillsborough, North Carolina, adds a parent's perspective:

> The things that homeschoolers miss out on [for example, football games, passing notes in class, and riding the bus] are so insignificant compared to the things that school kids miss out on—time with their parents, the chance to love learning, fresh air and sunshine, a free childhood.—*Zach, homeschooling father, Hillsborough, NC*

Homeschoolers note that they also "miss out" on the less desirable aspects of school. For example, a striking number of kids, when asked what they liked about homeschooling, said, "I like that I don't have to get up early." Freedom, in a variety of forms, turns out to be very important to homeschooled kids and parents and will be discussed at greater length in the next section.

In trade for any rituals homeschoolers do "miss," they get two things just as fun and utterly invaluable: *time* and *freedom*.

Time, Time, and More Time

In the absence of busy work, administrative tasks, class-changing, bus rides, attendance-taking, locker time, lunch lines, and so on, homeschoolers often get the following:

- time to play and be with friends
- time to have long talks and really get to know others
- time to swim, run, play, and practice sports
- time to be solitary
- time to pursue a learning experience or interest, including social ones, uninterrupted by bells, clocks, and homework

- time to get to know themselves
- time for traditional subject matter
- time to explore hobbies
- time to pursue talents, especially those not emphasized or valued highly in traditional school systems
- time to learn to live with siblings
- time to really talk with parents
- time to study
- time to *read freely*
- time to put on plays with friends
- time to travel
- time to sleep as much as needed

I'm twelve. I went to school in preschool, and then Mom didn't want me in school all day when I was only in first grade. .,. I like not having to get up early and go to school, not having any real tight schedule, being at home, being able to go over to friends' houses and stay and have overnights on weekdays. ... Being at home is just nicer than being in a classroom—I've got all my stuff, I can play my guitar, I can read and do stuff with [my brother]. ... I enjoy having my parents around, although sometimes they get tiresome. My friends and I usually skateboard, run around, do stuff on the computer, bike, [and the list goes on].—*Daniel, twelve-year-old homeschooler, Durham, NC*

Freedom, Freedom, and More Freedom

When I first wrote this book, I was going to mention in this chapter that some kids feel they have more freedom because of homeschooling. When I interviewed kids, though, I heard comments about freedom so frequently that it became obvious this was more than just a minor bonus; both kids and parents view freedom as a major benefit of homeschooling:

[I like homeschooling because] you're more free—you're not really free in school.

[His sister adds:] Like you have to sit at a desk and you sort of have to be silent and always do your work.

[Ricardo:] And you have to sit at a desk for seven and a half hours.—*Ricardo, nine-year-old homeschooler, Chapel Hill, NC*

[I like homeschooling because] it's nice to be—to feel—free.—*Marena, ten-year-old homeschooler, Durham, NC*

[The kids] are in on the decisions; it's not just, "We're the parents," and "Yes," or "No," and that's it. I think they realize that they have much more freedom than most of their peers.—*Laurie, homeschooling mother of two, Katonah, NY*

The advantages [of homeschooling] are many. The one we like most is the freedom. [My son] attended high school part time for three years (so he could run track), and [my other son] takes a community college class now. We tend to travel quite a bit, and a school schedule is extremely restrictive and difficult to work around, even on a day-to-day basis: getting up and there on time, making sure he gets picked up on time, [and so forth]. We like having the freedom to go where and whenever the spirit or circumstances move us!

Another biggie would be the time we get to spend together. This was actually the main reason I did it in the beginning. I just couldn't imagine sending my children off to be with other people for so many hours of the day. I also like the fact that my children get to move and do many things,

really be a part of our world, rather than spend loads of time at a desk, doing two-dimensional work. I like that they are making their own choices (though that can also qualify as a disadvantage).
—*Chris, former public school teacher and homeschooling mother of three (one now attending college), Michigan*

Of course, children do need to be exposed to serious and meaningful things, and this can happen while children feel completely safe, carefree, and not under pressure to rely on their own social savvy before they are prepared to. Childhood is a time in life when a person can be free and observe, take in, and learn about the world while living under the blanket of safety of parents who are in control and protect them. Indeed, this may arguably be the very reason children have parents at all. Many homeschooling parents believe that the safety net they provide actually facilitates their children's interest in and ability to explore and experience important pursuits and subject matters.

What else is childhood about, anyway? As a bumper sticker I read once said, "A happy childhood lasts a lifetime." Happy parenting!

chapter eight

BEING "COOL"

"When I use a word," Humpty Dumpty said in a rather scornful tone, "it means just what I choose it to mean—neither more nor less."

"The question is," said Alice, "whether you can make words mean so many different things."

"The question is," said Humpty Dumpty, "which is to be master—that's all."—Lewis Carroll, Through the Looking Glass

"When you're your own person and not so concerned with impressing, then the other person is very impressed."—Madonna

Defining "Cool"

W hen people ask about socialization, they may really be asking, "Is Johnny cool enough?" to which the return question must be asked: "What is 'cool'?" At a large homeschool play date I attended a few years ago, a school-going teenager who was visiting observed the homeschooled teenagers, who happily hung out with other teens, parents, and younger kids alike. Her reaction to them was, "They're so uncool!" The same day, while visiting the first session of a homeschool drama class, I heard a homeschooled boy saying of a new kid in class, "[He] is cool. When the teacher said to act like babies, everybody else crawled, and he was the only one who did something different."

These two children defined "cool" in very different ways, which raises the question of whether one was right and one wrong and whether there even is a definition for "cool." In search of more information about these questions, I discussed the issue of being "cool" with various homeschooled children, conventionally schooled children, and homeschooling parents. I discovered, interestingly, that homeschooled children seem to be less controlled by arbitrary, external ideas of what is "cool" and instead create their own definitions of cool that are actually more relevant to and in line with the real world.

Those who are concerned that a homeschooled child might not be "cool" are, most likely, mainly concerned about the child's well-being; that is, they want the child to be cool so that he can be happy. But what if being cool requires doing things that don't feel good or right or that are not in the child's best interests? When someone else defines "cool," it may require acting less smart or concerned about academics than you are (as it did in my case), or doing something dangerous to your health or safety, such as drugs, sexual activities, risky automobile behavior, and more. When being viewed as "cool" requires certain vices, going along with the crowd, taking unwise risks, a certain amount of sacrificing of self and values, hiding or suppressing intelligence or enthusiasm for learning, and so on, it is not necessarily something that serves our children well. Is this really something we want for our children? On the other hand, if children can grow up liking themselves, feeling confident, and knowing how to make good decisions, this is indeed something that will serve them well both during childhood and in adult life. If it is possible to be considered "cool" for possessing these qualities—individuality, intelligence, wisdom, a sense of morality, and self-worth—then this would be even better.

Either way, it seems clear that children define "cool" differently in a school vs. a homeschool setting. Angela, the teacher and former homeschooling mother mentioned previously, makes these observations about the "cool" phenomenon in school (names and some identifying details in the following account have been changed):

> What I see a lot of the time is the children who are the "cool" ones are most of the time the ones that have all sorts of problems, and their way of getting attention is by being the cool one. And you see these other children who are the more naïve, the more taken-care-of children. They look up to these others as cool [and think], "I want to imitate that." They want to imitate their vocabulary, they want to imitate the way they dress, and you're going, "Oh, that's the wrong role model. You don't want that role model." And as a teacher, I can't sit there and tell them—I can give them some education as far as character development and character education, which we're supposed to do, but you can only do so much.
>
> I feel that when you're homeschooling your child, you have more control as a parent over who your child's going to socialize with so that when they do socialize, they're socializing in a good, honest way, and they're developing their character in a way that you feel is appropriate. Later in life, you have developed your character, you know who you are, and hopefully you already are confident

131

in who you are. And then you can go out and socialize and see others and see what's right and what's wrong. Then you can make better choices than you can as a child.—*Angela, teacher (and former homeschooling mother)*

Homeschool Cool

The "cool" phenomenon doesn't seem to happen the same way among homeschoolers. Homeschooled children do describe each other and themselves as "cool," but it seems to carry a completely different meaning to them than it does to the typical school-going child. For one thing, in a traditional school setting, often only a select few children achieve "cool" or "popular" status. In a homeschool setting, there seems somehow to be more room for people to be considered cool. Perhaps this is partly a result of growing up feeling accepted rather than pressured to fit in—a difference many homeschoolers I interviewed have observed.

Acceptance

It seems that homeschoolers are often accepted by other homeschoolers regardless of clothing, physical appearance, age, socio-economic status, race, and so on. All homeschoolers are going against the grain, and individuality seems to be valued. Since there is no "tracking" and no inherent competitive nature to homeschool groups, kids seem less concerned with comparing and judging one another.

Stephen, a twelve-year-old who has been homeschooling for three years, comments on differences he noticed when he left school:

I figured out my friends that I found in homeschooling are a whole lot better than the ones I had in school. Nicer, I have to say. There is nothing that the other kids judge you by, like what you wear, or anything like that.

Not in homeschooling. School kids do judge you a whole lot worse than the homeschool kids.

In school I also felt under pressure to do things. ... It had to do more with what my friends did, and I went along with it. They did things that I didn't want to do, but they did it anyway, so I did it. That doesn't really happen in homeschooling. I don't know [why].

Also at school, I never really met anyone who wasn't good looking who was considered cool. Clothes had something somewhat to do with it, but some people didn't care, and [that's] just funny, I guess. Cool is just categories, basically. In school there were some people who were considered geeks, some were cool, some just no one talked about, they were just there. In homeschool there are no categories, because there's no school. Nobody cares. In my school, there's nobody to compete with, it's just me and my sister, and nobody judges the other person. —*Stephen, homeschooled twelve-year-old, Efland, NC*

James, homeschooling father of three, makes his own observation of this phenomenon:

You know, by second grade [in school] the cliques had formed. By second grade there was a group of people who were, "Okay, these people are friends together and I'm not in that group," kind of thing. And I don't get the same feel now with [homeschooling]. [My son] hangs out with [his friends] a bunch, but it's not the same kind of feel. It's not like, "We're cool, you're not." They just know each other better, and they're closer in age than some of the other kids that hang out together, but it never feels the same—exclusive might be the word. I appreciate it more, because they get more friends, and there's not that kind of exclusive like, "I'm this person's friend and that means I can't be this person's friend" or something like that.

And I've noticed that for some reason we seem to be able to make friends, too, with the public school kids that nobody's friends with. There's the kid up the street who's twelve and has some form of autism or something, and you can just tell that at school he is not the kid that people hang out with. He doesn't get invited over to [the school kids'] houses, and the homeschool kids—they don't care. They don't put that on him. They're just like, "You know, [he's] just another kid. Yeah, he's a little older [and] he doesn't really act it yet, but who cares?" I think [it's] because they get exposed to so many different kinds of people—they get exposed to more different kinds of kids. It's partially, too, that it's not the kids always defining what's cool and what isn't. They just don't see the differences as that important. It's like the clothes. I don't ever get the "we need the latest greatest Nike tennis shoe" kind of thing. It seems like there's less peer pressure on the kids because there's not as much structure on them.

There's not as much hierarchy going on, and pecking order and all of that, in their life. There's not nearly as many A's, B's, C's, D's, pluses, S's, (unsatisfactory, satisfactory)—they're not getting that. They don't view the world as, "Okay, let's grade this out." Their whole educational experience is not like, "Okay, let's look at this thing and put it in its rank order from worst to best." It's not, "Okay, math is the best subject, and doctors are the best profession." What's important to them is what's important to *them*. It's not about it being better; it's like, "This is what *I* am. What you like is good for you, what I like is good for me." It's not about somebody telling you, "This is better for you because I say so."

The schooling thing has such a structure to it that you get a whole caste system going: A students, D students, the music people, the science people—oh, heaven forbid you're a music *and* a science person. You get all that structure. And you internalize it. And I don't think these [homeschool] kids do that. They don't look at somebody else and say, "Is he uncool, is he somebody that I could have fun with, is he somebody I want to be friends with?" They don't look to another group and say, "What will all the other A students think; what will all the other science students think?" [Homeschoolers] don't feel that kind of thing.
—*James, homeschooling father of three, Durham, NC*

This alternative structure may ultimately be better preparation for social interactions in the "real world," where an ability to get along with many people, accept differences, be kind, be interesting, and be wise—not just wear a particular brand of shoes—is relevant for success in relationships.

Defining Their Own "Cool"

It is clear from talking to many homeschoolers that they don't feel enslaved by an external dictate of "cool" or a need to conform to one.

"I don't feel like it's important to be considered cool, because I just like to be who I am," says Lucinda, a homeschooled eleven-year-old from Durham, North Carolina, echoing the statements of many other homeschoolers. And when they do use the term "cool," they tend to define it for themselves:

I define people as cool when I like them and

they're nice, not if they're stylish or popular or something like that. As a matter of fact, there's not really a big popular cliquey thing in homeschooling. Most people that would be considered cool [at school] get on my nerves.

I think anyone in the world can be cool. In someone else's eyes, in their own eyes, just whatever.—*Corrin, homeschooled eleven-year-old, Durham, NC*

I recently overheard my own five-year-old daughter, Sadie, saying sadly to her brother, "I want to have cool-person pants like you, Saul. And a cell phone. I want to be cool, too!"

Saul, age nine, replied, "Let me tell you something, Sadie. You *are* a cool person. You don't have to wear cool-person pants to show it. You are a cool person no matter *what* you're wearing."

Later, I asked him what, in his opinion, makes someone cool. Shrugging, he said simply, "They're cool. Cool people set trends."

Of course, many people, schooled or not, might agree with the statement that trend-setters are "cool." It is interesting to note, then, that today's homeschoolers are themselves setting a trend. In other words, homeschooled children today are growing up in an environment that prepares them quite fully for a life in which trend-setting is not feared in the least.

Kids Feel Good About Being Homeschooled

Evidence suggests that kids like living in this different environment. Corrin, the homeschooled eleven-year-old quoted previously, tells how she feels about homeschooling versus when she was in school:

People can ask you, "Wouldn't you rather be in school with all the friends?" And I have just as many friends if not more than I would have in school. I think that I would be able to bear school, but I like homeschooling a lot better. What I really like about homeschooling is that you can work at home and at your own pace. You also don't have to deal with some of the pressures that come along with being in school, like just pressure to do things that are "cool," like basically dressing or speaking or whatever.

[When I was in school], people thought I was weird because of my name; it wasn't everybody else's name in the whole school—I wasn't Katie, I wasn't Sarah, I wasn't Alex. [Now that I'm homeschooled], for some reason I spend a lot less time obsessing over something—obsessing over whether the teacher will like it or whether the kids will like it. ... It's me! I'm at home in me.—*Corrin, homeschooled eleven-year-old, Durham, NC*

And a homeschooling mother of one from Massachusetts says:

I have been homeschooling my son, eleven years of age, for two years now. It was his choice to be schooled at home, he is a very athletic, outgoing child who enjoyed great popularity and success at school, but chose this route anyway.

At a recent homeschool group play date, I observed a seven-year-old child wearing a rather unique outfit. Certainly it was different from anything the other kids were wearing. It included a very small paisley tuxedo vest, a belt made of a yellow shoe-string, and a Tamagochi-type toy he pretended was a computer hanging from his "belt." The child was clearly proud of the original, functional outfit he had created. Though I was surprised he was wearing that (and a little concerned about how the other kids would react), he showed no concern at all about wearing such an outfit to the play date, where at least twenty other kids were present. And it seems he knew his social setting well; to my surprise, several kids complimented him on his unusual clothing. He also received several genuinely curious inquiries about his "computer" and not one jeer, sneer, jab, or negative look or comment of any kind.

In fact, the child had a marvelous time at the play date, played with lots of old friends and made one or two new ones. He went home feeling happy and satisfied with his fun-filled day and probably feeling at least somewhat affirmed for his individuality. I remember thinking that had he been in second grade at school, this would have been a very different day indeed.

At any rate, this particular seven-year-old, when he wants to, knows how to match his clothes. If as he gets older it becomes beneficial to him to dress more conventionally, he will no doubt do so. I have seen homeschooled teenagers who transferred to public school choose to dress and act in particular ways to "fit in" and be popular in school, with great success. Homeschooled children, who can easily observe the behavior and appearances of those around them, are perfectly capable of conforming *if they want* to. (Conforming, though, it must be noted, is not necessarily what makes a happy or successful adult.) Meanwhile, they are, for the most part, enjoying happy childhoods, feeling cool, being who they want to be, and learning that, after all, that's an okay thing to be.

chapter nine

RELATIONSHIPS WITH OTHER ADULTS

"I was a young person once, shortly after the polar ice caps retreated, and I distinctly recall believing that virtually all adults were clueless goobers."
—Dave Barry

One of the common images conjured about homeschooling is that of a child who has no adult influences other than his parents. Of course, this hypothetical situation entails all sorts of problems—the child never hearing any other views, perhaps not knowing what is "normal," never being able to separate from parents, and so on.

But, like so many fears about homeschooling, this one, too, is a product of the general misunderstanding present in our culture of what homeschooling is. Knowing that homeschoolers live and learn in the general community, gather and work with other families, and engage in lots of real-world activities, informed citizens can rest assured that homeschooling easily allows kids to have the influence of other, non-parental adults. In fact, homeschooling affords kids the unique opportunity to have real, meaningful relationships with various adults, and this benefits them in many ways.

To begin with, homeschoolers have the opportunity to form relationships with various adults in the community and to enjoy and learn from them in a situation that allows the adults to be allies, friends, and mentors rather than adversaries, disciplinarians, assigners of work, and judges of progress. David Guterson, in *Family Matters*, points out that most homeschooling parents, realizing that it is important for their kids to have relationships with other adults, go out of their way to create opportunities for such relationships to develop. "Ironically," he says, "it is homeschooled children who stand the better chance of moving beyond the home and into the lives of adult mentors" (Guterson 1992). Indeed, a great many homeschoolers are involved in mentor-type relationships with adults in the community through internships, classes, part-time jobs, skill-sharing, and the list goes on. In addition, many homeschooled kids develop close friendships with other parents in homeschooling communities that they spend time with.

The relationship dynamic school-going students have with teachers and other school personnel has social implications, too, and is an important part of their healthy or unhealthy social development. A great many teachers do their very best to support and encourage the creativity, individuality, and social development of their students. Many would like to know their students better and thereby do better for them. But they cannot avoid the simple but significant fact that they hold the grade book and must maintain discipline in a classroom full of children. In a system that by its very nature requires students and teachers to be in an essentially adversarial relationship—and to adhere to standardized behaviors, curricula, subject matter study, learning schedules, and "right and wrong" answers even on creative subject matter—the efforts of even the most dedicated, enthusiastic, and caring teachers are often frustrated. For teachers guiding the education of a class of twenty or more kids, there simply is not time or freedom, in the vast majority of school settings, to develop meaningful, one-on-one relationships with their students or to truly get to know each student as an individual. Schools are overcrowded, curricula must be covered, and test scores must be raised. As our governments "crack down" on education and "accountability," this becomes even more the case.

Angela, a public school teacher and former homeschooling mother of two, explains (names and some identifying details in the following account have been changed):

> The barrier to individualizing is that you have twenty-eight kids in the classroom. I can't give each one the time that they need. And I also have state standards. And they need to take that test, and if they don't do well, the school looks very bad. I could lose my job if my class doesn't do well; that's the point where it is. So that makes it very difficult in really helping each child the way they should be helped.—*Angela, former homeschooling mother of two*

Another public school teacher, Chris, who is from Michigan, explains similarly why she decided to homeschool her own children:

> I felt I had made an unfortunate discovery during my experience as a teacher—that the system is not set up with the children's best interests at heart. I had to deal, on nearly a daily basis, with an administration, federal laws, and even senior teachers who thwarted my efforts,

time and again, to attempt to make things better for my students. I didn't want my children put in a situation where they would be seen not as individuals with unique strengths and needs, but as part of a larger unit, seen perhaps as a liability or benefit to the organization. I also felt very strongly that no child should be trapped in a school building, the same room even, for so many hours each day. The deleterious social climate that can develop among thirty pupils of the same age was also a concern to me.

That said, please know that I do not doubt that there are some truly fantastic teachers out there making a difference in kids' lives. I just wasn't willing to put my kids through a twelve-plus year experiment in hopes of running into one or two of those teachers!—*Chris, former public school teacher and homeschooling mother of three, Michigan*

Likewise, teachers are not at liberty to develop meaningful, one-on-one relationships with their students, even if it were realistic for them to do so. Angela goes on to explain this dilemma (names and some identifying details in the following account have been changed):

You want to form a relationship with them and show them that you really care about them, but it's a fine line, because they're not yours, and you have to know where your place is as a teacher. You have to realize, "What I do in the classroom and the love and the motherliness that I give them in the classroom can only be to a certain point," because there's so many consequences. You can't touch them, you can't say certain things to them, because you never know what can be said by the child. You never know what situation that can get you into. ... You do want them to trust you, you do want them to feel comfortable with you and feel that the classroom is a home where they can be comfortable, but you also have to [maintain] a line and say you don't want them to be too comfortable either, because you don't know what consequences can come about from that. You can't get too involved, because sometimes you as an outsider don't know what's the best thing for that child, either.—*Angela, public school teacher, former homeschooling mother of two*

Moreover, in the school system, kids have a new teacher each year (and even each hour), lots of structured material to cover, and a teacher who must maintain order in a classroom of twenty or thirty. Such a system discourages meaningful, one-on-one attachment. Unfortunately, it is a downward spiral, since children thrive best both academically and socially when their individual needs are recognized, respected, addressed, and met. Schoolteacher and homeschooling father David Guterson discusses this in his book *Family Matters* and explains it with great eloquence—well worth reading.

One homeschooling mother shares her view on the matter:

Why did we take the kids out of school, specifically public school? My son was learning a skill that would not serve him at all well in life. He was learning to make himself invisible. With twenty-eight to thirty-two students per classroom, his young teachers ignored the five to ten kids in each class who were neither trouble-makers nor in the advanced learning group. Consequently, he stayed in the class, did his work, asked only the rare question, and ... well, he demanded nothing and that is exactly what he got. In both of his grades, the more experienced teachers had "retired"—usually early—and only the newer, less savvy teachers remained. They simply did not have the experience, the desire, or the capability to bring out the spark and excitement in a boy like [my son]. My daughter can probably make it, and make it well, in any school setting. But my husband and I strongly believe in a shared family experience. Accordingly, when we recognized the necessity and desirability of homeschooling our son, we determined that it was the better path for our daughter as well.—*Jane, homeschooling mother of two, Hopkins, Minnesota*

In a homeschool setting, not only do parents have time to get to know and attend to each child's individual needs and personality, but the children also have the freedom to get to know other adult members of the family and community who may or may not be required to behave as authority figures or juggle responsibility for numerous other children and tasks.

Steven, a homeschooling father in rural Mebane, North Carolina, tells about the many ways in which his son interacts and benefits from other adult members of the community:

Currently, Monday, Tuesday, and Thursday he's with a fellow learning about the horses and the chickens, but that's going to be changing soon because [this man] is going to be moving out of the community. Monday afternoons he's with me; I teach geography. He does spelling with [a close family friend] twice a week. He watches a Hindu epic with his godmother twice a week, and he's with his godfather one day a week, Thursdays he's at the homeschool group play date, Sundays he goes to church with [his mother], Wednesday afternoon he has aikido, so it's pretty templated out. And it changes; there are all sorts of other variables, but we find that the actual amount of time spent on academics is a fraction of what it would be in school.—*Steven, homeschooling father of one, Mebane, NC*

Because academics take so little time, homeschooled kids also have *more* time to develop relationships with the adults that all children have in their lives. One mother tells of the many adults serving as accessible role models in her son's life:

> He has ... neighbors who are real close—he interacts with them. He takes tae kwon do, so he has several adult masters he interacts with on a day-to-day basis. [He also has] aunts and uncles, grandparents, [and the list goes on].—*Missy, homeschooling mother of two, Cary, NC*

Another mother tells how other members of the family have developed close relationships with her son by participating in the homeschooling experience:

> [My son] often travels with my brother. They've gone to Jacksonville, Florida, and they've gone up to Baltimore. Last year they went up to Pittsburg. He spends a lot of time with my brother, and my brother lives in New York. I also feel like, in terms of education, my father has been very involved and has been a big influence. My father taught him how to write, and my brother taught him mathematics.—*Marianne, homeschooling mother of one, Boynton Beach, FL*

Discipline

Discipline by parents and by any other adult who enforces it is also part of the socialization process that children go through. At home, methods and attitudes toward discipline can be carefully chosen and implemented by the child's parents, but in school they are often chosen and carried out by miscellaneous adults who may or may not have any natural authority over the child and may or may not be in a position to understand (or care about) the child's unique situation. Because of the size and nature of the institutions, much of this discipline is based on fear, stress, and punishment, perhaps making it even more difficult for the children to develop positive relationships with the adults in their charge.

Even so, because children so crave and need relationships with adults, and because teachers know that this kind of relationship is valuable, kids do sometimes manage to develop meaningful relationships with a special teacher in spite of the system making this more difficult.

Respect and Natural Authority

One concern parents sometimes have about children's socialization is that they develop a healthy respect for authority. To some this may mean always obeying all elders and "superiors" (those holding a higher rank or post of any kind). However, what appears to be a respect for authority is not always a true *respect,* but is often rather a fear that is translated into obedience *while in the "authority" figure's presence.*

In school all adults are to be considered authority figures, and therefore, authority, ultimately, has little meaning. Authority means nothing, and when teachers aren't looking, rules are often not obeyed. It may be that this dynamic actually interferes with learning respect for authority, since the adults who kids are supposed to obey and respect in school lack the *natural authority* that exists in a parent who cares for the child's well-being and has taken care of that child over a long period of time. John Gray, Ph.D., in his book *Children*

Are From Heaven, explains the concept of natural authority. True respect comes from experiencing authority figures (for example, adults in charge) as benevolent, helpful, and wise figures who are respected because they are worthy of respect (Gray 1999). The respect expected in school is not true respect for authority because true respect for authority, like all true respect, must be earned. Parents naturally earn the respect of their kids by spending years loving and taking care of them and demonstrating that they indeed have the child's best interests in mind. General respect for authority may well grow out of a childhood in which parents are repeatedly observed to be benevolent and make wise decisions that prove beneficial to the concerned parties.

It is interesting to note the relationship between the words "authority" and "author"—the creator of a book or story. Authority in that case is the state of having *created.* On the other hand, being the "authority" on something also means one's word is trusted because she has studied the subject matter at length and *knows* it very well—perhaps better than anyone else and certainly better than most. In this sense, authority itself comes from knowing something well and perhaps in some cases from having created it. Just as God, the creator (who also knows all), is considered the highest authority of all (His word is both trusted and obeyed) according to Judeo-Christian religions, so too is the parent the highest earthly authority for a child. Because of both being the child's creator (or raiser) and knowing the child better than anyone else, the parent is naturally trusted by the child, who also naturally wants to please. Though many teachers and other school personnel are skilled at managing children, they cannot have the level of natural authority that a parent has.

To a certain extent, all adults, simply by virtue of being adults, *represent* parent or creator-figures and therefore have some degree of natural authority. However, this is subject to their behavior toward the child. When children perceive an adult to be other than benevolent, the adult loses a measure of true authority. In order to have true authority (in the sense that the child respects them), adults must demonstrate "grown-up" (mature and benevolent) behavior and that they have the child's interests at heart.

"Real" vs. "Artificial" Relationships

Some homeschoolers have raised questions about a distinction between "real" and "artificial" relationships.

Sarah, a mother of four lifelong homeschoolers (two are grown), describes the difference this way:

> Our children have always known where their feet were, always known where the ground was that held them. I've come to this theory that in school, whatever the school is, some portion of what you're doing is trying to figure out what the teacher wants of you. I have this image of Jell-O gelatin—heavy gelatin that you're standing on that wiggles a little bit. Or maybe an iceberg, floating. It's not stable, because [kids think], "I might want to think about what this topic is, but on top of that, I have to think about what it is *you* [the teacher] want me to be thinking about *about* this topic." And my kids have not had that. They have such a radar for—I wish I had a name for it—some sort of insincerity or inauthenticity, lack of authenticity of relationship there. They have such a radar. They do not tolerate any of that. They can smell it a mile off—inauthentic relationships. Where

[they think], "If you ask me a question, you're asking it to judge me, not in order to get the information. You are pretending to hold—or thinking that you hold—some power over me." And they know that they are in charge of themselves. They also are not so arrogant as not to look to others for guidance, but they're in charge of looking for that guidance.

I guess along those lines, what I figured out a long time ago was to never ask a question that I already know the answer to. And when I'm asked a question, I simply answer the question simply. And that's been pretty much what's guided us in our interactions with each other, which I guess I'm now calling "authentic interaction." So if I could encapsulate my homeschooling philosophy, that's what it is.—*Sarah, mother of four lifelong homeschoolers, Durham, NC*

And homeschooled children are often described as relating better to the adults they are in contact with. Why this is the case, I don't know. But it is a very common observation of homeschoolers that they are unusually comfortable with adults:

I did have many doubts along the way. Any parent wonders, "Have I done well enough?" But it was very clear to me many years ago that my kids already had the attributes from homeschooling that I wished they would have. Someone said to me recently, "Your children are the only ones who give me eye contact." They'll engage you. And I find that with other homeschoolers.—*Laurie, homeschooling mother of two, Katonah, NY*

The "true" relationships that homeschoolers are able to have with adults pay off for them in many ways. Guidance from figures of genuine authority is much more likely to be heeded, which will serve kids well as they move into positions of greater decision-making. Moreover, by having the opportunity to spend real time with adults in the community, kids stand to gain a great deal of information, wisdom, and even social know-how that could not be gained in a highly scheduled, regulated group situation. And finally, homeschooled kids may interact with a realistic range of adults—not all of whom are teachers or of the same socio-economic background, world-view, demographic, and so on.

chapter ten

DIVERSITY AND MINORITY SOCIALIZATION

"My goal in life is to find out about people."
—Saul, homeschooler, age seven

"We must become the change we want to see."
—Mahatma Gandhi

A neighbor, explaining her reservations about homeschooling, once said to me, "I want my kids to be exposed to the kinds of people you find in public school. Aren't most homeschoolers white, middle-class types?" Many other parents also express similar reservations regarding diversity issues associated with homeschooling.

This makes sense, since we perceive that homeschoolers do not spend time around as many people as conventionally schooled children. Importantly, though, it is not only the quantity but the *quality* of interaction that is important, especially for developing accepting and understanding attitudes toward diverse groups of people.

The idea of exposing our kids to diversity is very important to many American parents and citizens. It is one major concern that potential homeschoolers and real homeschoolers share about homeschoolers' socialization. Fortunately for all concerned, homeschooling can afford children plenty of exposure to diverse people and offers opportunities for children and families to experience quality interactions with various people in ways that are rarely possible in schools.

Opportunities for Exposure

One of the great ironies of the homeschooling debate is that the very parents who are hesitant to homeschool because they want their kids to be exposed to diversity are the very ones who would be most certain to ensure that it happened no matter what schooling situation they chose for their children.

It is indeed possible in homeschooling to grow up without much contact or interaction with people of other races, religions, socio-economic backgrounds, and walks of life. This is also possible, and common, in schools. But it is also possible, with homeschooling, to experience diversity in a way that is much more positive than is typically found in an institutional setting. The homeschool population is much more diverse than generally imagined.

Homeschoolers Are Diverse

The belief that all homeschoolers are from white, fundamentalist, conservative, middle-class families is pure fallacy. Research shows that the majority of homeschooling families are *not* doing so for religious reasons (Bauman 2001). Homeschoolers hail from all major religious backgrounds, as well as a wide range of income levels, political affiliations, cultural and racial backgrounds, and so on. Homeschooling support groups may contain a wonderful mix of individuals.

> I think my kids are exposed to diversity in our county; it is a wonderful place to homeschool. We have a big mix in our homeschooling groups and also in the church we attend (Unitarian Universalist). My kids are more socialized than many school kids I have seen. They aren't afraid to talk to people not their own age, race, religion, [and so on]. Here, anyway, there is actually a problem with too much socialization! It is totally understood if you call someone up and say, "We need a stay at home day today; we are burned out!"—*Sue, homeschooling mother of three, upstate NY*

In fact, the diversity of the homeschooling population is increasing rapidly. By 2003 in the US, in addition to the many associations and groups for homeschoolers in general, homeschool support organizations and Web sites had also sprung up dedicated specifically to African American homeschoolers, Islamic homeschoolers, Jewish, Latino, Hindu, Lutheran, Quaker, Seventh-Day Adventist, Pagan, Unitarian, Christian, Fundamentalist, Buddhist, Mormon, "special needs," single parent, vegan, Jehovah's Witness, Catholic, Native American, and even Native American Catholic homeschoolers (Lines 2000; Zeise 2005). These groups do not necessarily segregate themselves from one another, but the presence of these many support groups and resources reflects the growing diversity of the homeschooling population.

Why Minorities Are Turning to Homeschooling

The minority presence in the homeschooling community is growing at an amazing rate. According to Patrik Jonsson, about 120,000 African American children were homeschooled in 2003, or about 5 percent of the homeschooling population, a fact echoed by the African American Homeschoolers Network and other related resources (African 2003). This number is "up from a few thousand in 1998." Jonsson reports that "thousands of African American parents are homeschooling their kids in a growing backlash against America's public-education system—schools that many parents deem too dangerous, too judgmental, or just bad fits" (Jonsson 2003).

A survey of college students suggests that this trend will continue. Asked whether they would consider homeschooling their future children, almost half of black students responded they would or might homeschool, whereas less than a quarter of white students did (Lines 2000). In 2003 Jennifer James founded the National African-American Homeschoolers Alliance when her North Carolina organization for African American homeschoolers in the state was being contacted and joined by homeschoolers across the United States. She recognized an "urgent need" for resources to become available to people homeschooling African American children. Within a year and a half, over seven hundred families had joined her organization (www.naaha.com).

Many other groups have similarly developed to support the increasingly diverse homeschool population, including the types of organizations listed above. There is no question that diverse homeschoolers are "out there." It can take some effort for new homeschoolers to find and connect with these diverse individuals, and fortunately, many homeschoolers are deeply committed to fostering relationships with a variety of people.

Francis, a thirteen-year-old from Florida, explains why diversity is important to him:

> If you can't tolerate other people, then what can you do? You can't change if you can't tolerate others. You can only force yourself to be one way, rather than being able to change your mind.
> —*Francis, thirteen-year-old homeschooler, Boynton Beach, FL*

Racism and Prejudice in Schools

For many families, schools are not turning out to be the havens of integration and tolerance that many had hoped. According to an article by Johanna Wald (found at www.salon.com), the "zero tolerance" policy that went into effect in public schools nationwide in 2001 "has resulted in disproportionate punishments and racial profiling." This may be evidence of what Russ Skiba (as quoted in the article) calls a "pervasive and systematic bias" against minority children in public schools. Wald says the zero tolerance problem has drawn to many people's attention the observation that "a parallel tracking system is in effect in our nation's schools: one feeding mostly white, affluent and middle class students to college, the other feeding poor, minority kids to prison" (Wald 2001).

Moreover, "racial buffering," whether intentional or accidental, is also possible (and common) in school. Kids are "tracked," grouped into cliques, and so on. As a result, they don't have much opportunity to socialize with one another. School children tend to be in schools with kids from their same geographic (and thus socio-economic) areas, and those who are bussed to other areas for the purpose of making the schools more heterogeneous are often "tracked" into separate class groups within the school. All over the US, educators recognize the negative social implications of tracking (Guterson 1992). In addition, schools often inadvertently encourage exclusive or separatist behavior toward children different from oneself. David Guterson observes: "Ten years ago I taught at a public high school much celebrated for its diversity, an inner-city school with a voluntary busing program widely hailed as a model of integration. As it turned out my Advanced Placement Senior English class was uniformly composed of upper-middle-class white students who were quite frank in discussing the mechanisms they had devised for fending off others in the school" (Guterson 1992). Of course, schooling situations vary in this regard, and some are no doubt better than the one Guterson describes in terms of racial relations.

Still, it is no wonder that more and more minority families are turning to homeschooling to find a different environment where their kids can live and learn. A spokesperson for the African American Homeschoolers Network says, "Public schools in urban cities (where many of us live and work) are not providing our children with quality education. In many of the schools, physical violence is an everyday occurrence. Psychological warfare is ever-present. How can children learn and grow to their full potential in these hostile environments?" Another group, the Afrocentric Homeschoolers Association, "seeks to dispel racist myths, self-destructive beliefs, and the propagation of stereotypes through self-education. ... Through anti-racist, Black-positive homeschooling, we empower our children to live well as adults" (Afrocentric 1996). The National African-American Homeschoolers Alliance is spearheading a campaign encouraging black families to cut their television viewing in half, in hopes of improving the educational achievement and learning capacity of these children (NAAHA 2003). There is no doubt about it: black families want better for their children, and they are finding that homeschooling is one way to get it:

> I was worried about racism. [My husband is black.] About teasing and shunning from the other students and prejudicial treatment from both students and teachers. My intention was to help them to avoid this as much as possible, especially while they were very young.
>
> Of course, racism isn't just in the schools; it's everywhere. I like to think I protected them from a small but concentrated and possibly continual assault. They've experienced reactions in public since they were babies. Much of this is due to ignorance and poor social graces rather than outright racism.
>
> As they grew, they were exposed to racist comments from neighborhood children and even from their friends. When I knew about these instances, we could talk about them with the child and parents involved. But the instances were few and not too noticeable until the boys reached their mid teens. When my oldest attended a large suburban high school part time, he was asked on his first day who does he *hang with* (white or black). I was proud of his answer, which was something along the lines of, "I choose my friends by their character, not their color." As he was not visibly bruised, I guess it worked out okay!
>
> [My son] has had some run-ins with persons of authority (security guards, police) assuming he was not entitled to be in the place he was or worse: a wanted drug dealer! I know I don't even hear about most incidents of racism that they

encounter, but they have strong senses of identity and self confidence, which I think serves them well in dealing with these issues.

I'm not certain that they would have come out of public school with this strong sense of self. I think it is more likely that an unnatural drive for self preservation could have created an inflated defensive stance and a chip on the shoulder or worse: feelings of unworthiness, being downtrodden, and being unable to achieve their dreams.—*Chris, former public school teacher and homeschooling mother of three, Michigan*

Other Minorities Are Turning to Homeschooling, Too

But it's not just the families of African American kids who seek a better environment for their minority children. The Native American Home School Association, at its Web site, states in bold print, "We Have The Right To Be Who We Are." It says, "There were times when our children were forced from us to government regulation schools or off reservation religious schools, to learn things that OTHER people thought that they should know. ... Today there is support and LEGAL assistance available for those who want to homeschool." This organization is working on its own alternative curriculum guidelines, which would reflect both state requirements and Native American areas of study. The Web page ends with the strong words: "Because they are our children, that's why!" (Native 2003). Another group, Native Americans for Home Education (NAHE), believes that "Native American children can learn and grow best at home, while preserving their heritage and culture, which seems to be diminishing so quickly in this time of modernization and progress." They seek to provide support in the form of curricula, Web sites, activities, book fairs, pow wows, chat groups, and legal information. They also strive to help preserve the heritage and traditions of the "First Nations" (NAHE 2003).

Many other minority groups, finding themselves inadequately supported and educated by the schools, are also finding a home in homeschooling. And many "majority" families also count the avoidance of a racist school environment among their reasons for homeschooling, as well.

Attitudes Toward Diversity

Ultimately, though, in any educational situation, it is the attitudes and motivation of the *parents* that largely determine and inform a child's exposure, education, and attitudes toward diversity. Just as school systems are adopting special curricula to teach tolerance, so can (and do) many homeschool families emphasize or encourage tolerance, understanding, and acceptance of differences. Take for example the Daughters of Earth Homeschool, an organization that existed a few years ago in Virginia. Its Web site described it as "Home Education With Universal Consciousness," offering to their own family as well as to the homeschool community at large "grassroots support for International Families with emphasis on embracing diversity and respect for our many cultures."

One homeschooling mother shares her view on diversity:

> To me there are so many axes of diversity—
> there's diversity of race (which is one of the ones
> that we think of traditionally), or diversity of
> culture, and there's diversity of class. There are
> so many axes. [My kids] are exposed to a range of

homeschooling from unschooling to structured curricula, but ... I guess in some ways I would say that there's not a huge amount of diversity, and that's one of the things that I keep my ear out for—opportunities to make that possible.

But there's diversity you embrace. I'm willing for my children to be exposed to the reality that there are people who are racist or bigoted, but I'm not interested necessarily in having that be a part of our community. That would send the message to my children that that's something I find acceptable or valued. I think I can step back far enough to recognize that there's [some kinds of] diversity out there that I'm not interested in. [I can also recognize] there's diversity that is appealing or of value and also that somebody might be able to open my eyes to the fact that there's some diversity that is of value that I don't currently think is of value. Well, for one example of the diversities that I value in our group is that we have lesbian parents in our group, so if [my daughter] hits fourteen and suddenly realizes she's attracted to women, that's in the sphere of the range of what she's experienced as being part of our acceptable—you know, she's not getting messages that that's not acceptable.

I wouldn't want to miss out on some diversity that I felt was totally acceptable but just didn't happen to happen in my life—ranges of people who I would be totally comfortable with but just don't end up in my circle. So those are the ones that I try to listen out for and make sure that if there's an opportunity [I take it]. That or biracial parents—I'm very willing to have that be influenced, to have my eyes and my heart opened to that. This is not a piece of our community that I have a history of being connected to, but it's one that I'm perfectly happy to stretch a little bit and include. Hispanic stuff is one of the pieces to me that's like this growing, huge piece, and it's to be reckoned with in some form. So [I'm] trying to make that open; Let's figure out ways to bridge that, as my kids are gonna grow up in a different climate than I have.—*Elizabeth, homeschooling mother of two, Hillsborough, NC*

Quantity vs. Quality of Interactions

It may indeed be the case that homeschoolers do not encounter the same quantity of "minority" or other kids as school-going children do, since schools often have minority students bussed in and so on. Homeschoolers may have a smaller number of friends or acquaintances of different backgrounds from their own. When homeschoolers interact with people from other walks of life, it is often in "real-life" contexts: while running businesses, while patronizing businesses, as mentors or apprentices, and so on.

It is not just the quantity but the *quality* of these interactions that makes up a child's education about diverse people. Interacting with diverse individuals in a real-life setting may encourage children to see them as "real people" at work and play rather than as hordes of "others" or as a "them" in an institutional setting.

Though schools have been integrated, for example, for many years racism and various other "isms" continue to abound in America. To once again quote David Guterson, "Those who would make much of schools as the breeding ground of social understanding should think again about the adult world schools have helped create. Shall we give schools credit for holding the line while the fabric of society unravels around us, or shall we name schools as a contributor?" (Guterson 1992). Many parents do not want their kids exposed to the racist attitudes so often found in schools and seek a new way to introduce their kids to diversity. Many of them are finding this new way in homeschooling.

With homeschooling it is possible to take advantage of the time and freedom this lifestyle affords to have true and meaningful contact with diverse individuals, to an extent that may be unavailable to most school children.

In homeschooling there is no "tracking," and there seems to be less cliquish and other exclusive behavior. In the homeschool group I visited that first day, there were fifty or more families. Among those families were kids of gay parents and straight parents, kids of white and black parents, kids with stay-at-home dads and employed dads, with stay-at-home moms and employed moms, there were kids whose parents lived in large houses and drove expensive cars, and kids whose families were scraping by. There were Jewish, Christian, Muslim, Unitarian, inter-faith, atheist, agnostic, and families who practiced their own personal kinds of spirituality. There were people who used formal curricula and those who unschooled and everything in between. All the kids were friends, and I never observed anyone ridiculing, excluding, or otherwise mistreating anyone else on the basis of these factors. These diverse children were brought together by the fact that they were homeschoolers. Their differences did not seem to interfere with their friendships, because understanding and acceptance was promoted in all aspects and modeled by the parents.

When parents are present and know their children's friends well, they are able to offer much guidance to the children on the matter of acceptance— an issue that may be dear to the hearts of people raising their children in a less common way. Parents can and often do encourage acceptance and real relationships between their children and others.

Of course, homeschoolers do not socialize only with other homeschoolers. They socialize with the world at large and have similar opportunities to engage in positive interactions and learning experiences with non-homeschooling members of the community. Diversity is not just in schools. It is everywhere.

Diversity Is All Around Us

People of all ages, sizes, shapes, religions, races, political affiliations, socio-economic backgrounds, and so on are out walking the streets, running and working in local businesses, living in our neighborhoods, working out at the gym, reading at the library, being featured in the news, and so forth. Also, in addition to the opportunities that exist in the immediate community, homeschoolers have a much greater freedom than most to travel to other places, and as a group they tend to do so. Regardless of where our children are educated, it is the way we teach and the understanding, acceptance, and ability to learn that we bring to our interactions with different people that informs our children's attitudes. And it is not just the quantity of different people but the *attitudes* we model and thereby instill in our children about these differences that are the real issue:

> [My son] has noticed for quite some time now that people come in all shapes and colors, and we try to express that it's not what's on the outside or how a person looks or talks that is important; it's attitude, compassion, and what's on the inside that counts. We have quite a few handicapped people in our community, and he will often ask, "How did she get that way?" So I explain, "She may have been born like that, or she had a very bad accident that made her need to be in a wheelchair or walk with a severe limp." He then

of course asks, "Will they get better?" Sometimes I know the answer, sometimes I don't. Our homeschool groups have a diverse lot of people: Asian, African Canadian, American, German, Scottish, and the list goes on, so it gives ample opportunity to teach about the differences in people.

Lately we've been talking about God. It's a tough subject for me. Both my husband and I are Roman Catholic; however, I'm the only one who attends mass on a somewhat regular basis. I take the boys with me on occasion. [My son] asks many questions about God and Jesus. Recently he asked me why the priest doesn't have a wife and kids. Well, to be honest with you, I don't know, and I don't agree with this policy of the priests not marrying. I have yet to come up with a good explanation for this. I think I may just take [my son] to the church and ask Father to explain it to us.

The other kids he plays with from our group are a wide range of [religions]. We have Orthodox Jews, Presbyterians, Atheists, and Baptists. I enjoy listening to each Christian's faith stories. I find it very interesting learning how other people practice the same faith, and I try to pass this onto [my son] (and my husband) so that they can see how different, yet still alike, we all are in our beliefs.

Accepting differences in the human race is very important to me. It's the key to having a peaceful co-existence. As you can see, [my son] is more than exposed to diversity. I think it has a lot to do with the way we are as parents and our life styles that give our children this great opportunity to interact with many different people and cultures.—*Theresa, homeschooling mother of one, Ontario, Canada*

If we are out in the world day after day talking to people and living full, rich lives, rather than sitting in a classroom focused on one specific subject matter, we can have real opportunities to interact and get to know people. We can begin to see all these different individuals as real people, and then we can begin to truly understand, accept, and embrace our differences and similarities.

After all, this is what exposure to diversity is for, isn't it? And this is the kind of diversity available to homeschoolers who seek it.

chapter eleven

PREPARATION FOR THE "REAL WORLD"

"Schools and schooling are increasingly irrelevant to the great enterprises of the planet. No one believes anymore that scientists are trained in science classes or politicians in civics classes or poets in English classes. The truth is that schools don't really teach anything except how to obey orders."—John Taylor Gatto, New York State Teacher of the Year, 1990, Dumbing Us Down

"One should guard against preaching to young people success in the customary form as the main aim in life. The most important motive for work in school and in life is pleasure in work, pleasure in its result, and the knowledge of the value of the result to the community."—Albert Einstein

P eers, freedom, family, coolness, diversity, and time to be kids aside, there is another question that strikes doubt into the minds of many non-homeschoolers: "How can a child become prepared for life in mass society without growing up in a mass social setting like school?" Or, "How will they learn to be

167

functioning members of mass society without having to be functioning members of a mass schooling environment?" These are often-asked questions and very interesting ones indeed.

If someone argued that a prison inmate was getting better preparation for the outside world by being in prison (and surrounded mostly by other inmates) than an ordinary citizen could get by living in the outside world, people might understandably think this person was deluded or crazy. Yet the argument is often made that children confined to school every day are in a better position to learn skills for living in the "real world" than children who are not.

History has shown, and we shall see for ourselves, that homeschoolers, who are educated in the "outside" world rather than inside a classroom, function exceptionally well in the "real world."

Homeschoolers as Adults

A great deal of evidence supports the claim that homeschoolers end up very well prepared for the "real world." One study of adults who had been homeschooled as children found that none were unemployed, none were on welfare, and the vast majority believed homeschooling had helped them to become independent individuals and to interact with people from a variety of socio-economic backgrounds. They strongly supported home education (NHERI 2003). Also, homeschoolers have been admitted to and graduated from a wide variety of different colleges and universities, including Ivy League schools (www.learninfreedom.org).

In fact, historically, homeschoolers have been phenomenally successful at taking part and finding their place in the "real world." A formidable number of famous and important figures throughout history have been homeschooled. Among them are George Washington, Martha Washington, Abraham Lincoln, Woodrow Wilson, Mark Twain, Benjamin Franklin, Winston Churchill, Albert Einstein, Booker T. Washington, Will Rogers, Sally Ride, Orville Wright, Wilbur Wright, C.S. Lewis, Agatha Christie, George Washington Carver, Wolfgang Amadeus Mozart, Leonardo daVinci, Charlie Chaplin, Andrew Carnegie, Clara Barton (founder of the Red Cross), and many US governors, legislators, judges (including Supreme Court justices), Constitutional Convention delegates, and no fewer than ten of the forty-three US presidents (at the time of this writing). (See Appendix B for a longer list of famous homeschoolers.) Today, homeschoolers are still graduating from top colleges and universities around the nation and the world and proceeding on to bigger and better things, much of which we can as yet only imagine.

Madeline, a twenty-year-old college student who was homeschooled her whole life, sheds light on how homeschooling's unique nature prepared her to find her way in college and the real world:

> It was a really comfortable situation and that led to me being really comfortable with who I am and my choices. And I don't see that necessarily in most other people my age. I think that a lot of that has to do with how our public school system takes personal choice out of most of it. You do things because you have to do them, and you do them well because you think you should, and you're not necessarily spending your time doing things because you chose to do them. [Through homeschooling] I was given the opportunity to choose how I spent my time, in a lot of ways. I mean, if you said you were going to do something, you did it, and you definitely did your chores— you weren't let off easy all the time—but I

definitely made up my mind about why it was I was doing things. And I was asked to articulate that.

So when I got to Bennington [College], ... a lot of people struggle, because Bennington as an institution asks you to say why it is that you want to study what it is that you're studying, because they don't prescribe a course. So I was like, "Oh yeah, that's not hard for me, because I know that I can do this. I know that I decided to study these things for reasons that I know." And so I can put them out there and say it. And I know a lot of people who are struggling with the idea of knowing *why* they want to do something, knowing *if* they actually want to do something, because they haven't had experience making those choices for themselves.—*Madeline, twenty-year-old college student, homeschooled until college, Bennington, VT*

What most citizens don't realize is that homeschooled kids, free of insulation within the schoolhouse walls, *already* function within society on a day-to-day basis during their childhoods. While some may be too young to hold jobs, they daily observe and interact not only with other children but also with adults in the working world—visiting businesses, sometimes accompanying their parents to work, participating in volunteer work, and often acquiring jobs of their own during the teen years.

Madeline continues, describing what she was doing while her conventionally schooled peers were in a classroom:

I started doing student theater at Duke University when I was fifteen, so I'd seen a lot of the college scene before arriving at school [that is, college], and in a lot of ways I was done with a lot of it. I was like, "Yeah, okay, I've seen weekend parties." And so it wasn't novel. And the freedom you get when you're at [college] wasn't a novel idea to me. The people—it's their first time going anywhere without their parents. I had already gone off and done other things. I traveled in Europe for six months the year I was seventeen. [Before that], I was dancing about eighteen hours a week, mostly at Duke University, also in Raleigh—I was taking ballet and modern. I was working about ten to fifteen hours a week at the costume shop in a theater company and doing some theater work there, I was taking photography on and off, taking music lessons on and off, I was an assistant teaching drama classes at the Durham Arts Council, I started a theater company that happened in the summers, and my friend and I were editors for the children's newsletter that came out of the Haw River Festival.

I've had the opportunity to have a lot of real-world work experience, which a lot of people my age haven't had. Like in the theater, I've worked alongside a lot of professional crews, and I've seen how that works. I've lived in that environment, and a lot of people my age haven't because I got to do that when I was little—I had my days open. In a lot of ways, I have a lot of experience that somebody older than me would have. I think without that beginning, I wouldn't have had the job I have.—*Madeline, twenty-year-old college student, homeschooled until college, Bennington, VT*

In fact, a researcher named Dr. Montgomery (1989) found that homeschooled kids were equally involved in "extracurricular" activities commonly associated with future leadership as private school students and more so than public school students (NHERI 2003). Many homeschooled children own their own businesses; others often help with the family business, acquiring marketable skills that may actually give them a head start in the job market:

> I think homeschooling better equips children for the real world. They have more interaction with people outside of their peer group, and as a parent you have more control over who their friends are. They are more responsible. They also tend to have a better sense of the real world because they tend to be more involved in their community.
>
> [For example,] our [homeschool] support group was asked by McDonalds to decorate their windows for special holidays, which we did because the schools were too busy. Through our homeschool co-op we have had many requests for our homeschoolers to help in the community. Another benefit of homeschooling is that our children can be available during the day. Schoolchildren miss many [real-world] opportunities because they happen during the day while they are in school.—*Glenda, homeschooling mother of six (homeschooling for ten years), Ontario, Canada*

> I often take him on sales calls. What better thing can I teach him than how to meet somebody, help them with their needs, deliver the service, and deal with different situations every time? No matter what he's gonna do, he's going to have to deal with people. And there's nothing like seeing your parents do it.—*Steven, homeschooling father of one, homeschooling nine years, Mebane, NC*

It's not just jobs that are important in the real world, though; skills for healthy and responsible living are surely important, too, as are an awareness of cultural issues and a healthy sense of what is important in life:

> I liked homeschooling. I don't regret it. I guess there are always questions in any path that anyone chooses, but I feel like—and this is just my opinion—I got a different, more cultured upbringing [than people I see who go to school]. I feel like I'm more prepared for *living*. A lot of what's done in school is so *repetitive*, like busywork. Now that I'm in college, I've learned that in a lot of cases you just have to kind of cram the information into your head—though it's not really something you'll use in life, unless you have a very specific career. In homeschooling I was given the chance to spend time on things I love and not really drilled on busywork that I'm gonna forget anyway. I'm really thankful for that.
>
> This college I'm going to—a lot of people who attend it aren't quite as motivated as I am. They aren't really interested in being there. My feeling is, "What's the point of going if I'm not going to try and do well?" But they feel like they have no choice.—*Stephanie, eighteen-year-old college student, homeschooled until college, Katonah, NY*

> I've never been to school. I have gone and visited a day here and there to see what it's like. I realized it's not for me. I am very athletic, I like to move a lot, and homeschooling has given me freedom to do my athletics and to get the kind of education I want—not just a book education, but a *life* education. I feel more ready to be in the real world, because I get it not from a textbook, but firsthand. It's not all book smart that counts in life.—*Julian, fifteen-year-old homeschooler, Katonah, NY*

Society Now and Into the Future

One question thinking parents and citizens must ask is this: "Are our children best served by being prepared to function in society as it is now or society as it will be ten or twenty years from now?" Though homeschoolers do well in college, already even college has lost its status as the end-all-be-all goal in life for the current new generation. (For example, consider the number of start-ups headed by twenty-something citizens with no degrees in computer science or business.)

A Better, Freer-Thinking Culture

The historically significant homeschoolers listed above made enormous contributions to our culture. If they had been content to leave things the way they were, rather than looking forward to what the future could hold, they would not have made the important contributions they made to society. Instead, they knew that the world ten or twenty years down the road did not have to be the same as the world that particular day, and the purpose of life did not have to be to keep doing what was already being done. Perhaps they, like today's homeschoolers, were asked how they would "adjust" to society without going to school, but instead turned the tables and helped society "adjust" to gradually become what it is today. In the truest sense, they helped shape the future.

Perhaps we, too, can ask ourselves: "What *does* the future hold? Will it be the same, or different? And what do our children really need in order to be prepared for it?"

Homeschooling itself seems to encourage this kind of freer, forward-thinking approach to life.

Homeschoolers and their parents, in general, rather than trying to fit their lives into the usual mold, are instead using the world and their resources in the way that they have found to be best for themselves and their communities:

Someone said, "Reasonable men bend their will to the world; unreasonable men bend the will of the world to them." So all progress is made by unreasonable men. But that's it. I mean, these [homeschooled] kids learn to look at the world and say, "It's there for me to kind of shape the way I want to shape it." And school kids are like, "I need to fit into this shape that the world's in."

When you go to public school, you have to fit. You have to fit into the structure—you have to be there on time, you have to go home when they say, you have to get on the bus they say, you have to take the class they say when they say, write the story when they say, put the title where they say, stop when they say to stop. So even if you tried to duplicate that at home, you can't. Even if you said, "I'm gonna do eight to nine at the dining room table, I'm gonna sit them down, I'm gonna run them through the curriculum, and make them do this and that," [you won't be able to do it.] You'll necessarily shape what you're doing to your student more, because there are fewer of them and there's less structure.

[Homeschool kids] don't immediately throw things onto this hierarchy and structure that they've been forced into. They don't look at the world and say, "You know, this is better than this, this person is better than this person because this person knows science and this person can only sing. Or this person lives on a farm and this person lives in the city, and city life's obviously more sophisticated and better than rural or country life," or whatever. They just don't think of it that way. They don't see those gradations, whatever they are. Hierarchy requires structure.

But every person you've ever looked at who's made it to the top of this "hierarchy" is someone who just threw it out the window and broke every rule there was of the hierarchy and said, "Forget that. I'm not going to buy into all that, I'm just going to go to the top of it and do what I want to do. ... I'm just going to study exclusively violin. I could care less about fractions." And yeah, that seems really imprudent, and you're right, it's a great way to crash and burn. But you know what? They wind up at Carnegie Hall and make millions of dollars. Everybody you can point to that you say is "successful" circumnavigated that whole thing. Gates is one—Bill Gates is one. I don't know his entire biography history, but if I recall right, he didn't finish college. He went off and started a software company. And he didn't start from the bottom of the company and work his way up; he never had an entry-level job.

It happens in business a lot. From today: LeBraun James. If this guy's coming right out of high school and going into the NBA, you know that just doesn't fit. Even in an area where you know there's supposed to be that you go to four years of college, you get out, you go into the NBA, but guess what—he said, "Oh, forget that. I don't need the four years of structure and whatever you're talking about—I'm good enough right now outta high school to go right into this." And these guys are getting the biggest contracts of all. It's because they totally ignore the system as it's set up and say, "I'm gonna make my own set of rules. I'm gonna do what I wanna do, not what you tell me I *can* do." And that's the real difference: "I'm gonna do what I *want*. Not what I'm told, necessarily."

The [homeschool] kids make their own decisions—they get to decide what's important to them, and they're much more open (to me) to seeing the value in something that's not necessarily viewed as valuable. I really do think that's just the fact they're able to do that without being judged all the time.—*James, homeschooling father of three, Durham, NC*

What Is the Real World?

What even is the real world? Those words—the "real world"—are often associated with negative connotations: hard knocks, difficult lessons, going it alone. Some would no doubt say the competitive, peer-driven, "me-first" nature of school socialization is the way the *real world* is and that kids need preparation for that. But this may not be as true as it seems. Perhaps we choose our own lives and make our real world through our attitudes:

I think people define the real world as the harsh, dog-eat-dog aspect—the hard, lonely anonymity. That is *one* real world, but there are others.—*Zach, homeschooling father of two, Hillsborough, NC*

Culturally, we sometimes define the real world as the aspects of life that are harsh, and people with a highly positive or optimistic attitude are sometimes even described as not living in the "real world." But this logic is circular: the "real world" is considered harsh because whatever is harsh is considered like the "real world." It could be similar thinking that school is similar to the real world, because the term "real world" is applied to whatever is school-like.

In the complete real world, though, the social patterns and habits learned in school are not necessarily important or even relevant. Academically speaking, it is often observed that once you graduate, you never again use most of what you learned in school. The same is observed socially: that once you are grown up, it doesn't matter whether you were popular in school, the captain of the football team, the nerd, the kid with the cool shoes, or the geek with the hand-me-downs.

In the *real* real world, it is often the computer nerds of yesterday who are the successful entrepreneurs of today. The head cheerleader may turn out to be a beauty queen, a rocket scientist, or a junkie. The unnoticed child may become an entrepreneur, a teacher, a criminal, or anything else. It is probably the child's family life, mostly, that determines this. School socialization, ultimately, is really mostly just training for a *school* environment. Family and community-based socialization, on the other hand, is preparation for family and community living (in other words, for real life).

Put another way, one can be seen as preparation for a real world envisioned to be competitive, adverse, and everyone-for-himself and the other for a real world envisioned to include the potential for a life surrounded by loved ones and friends, within the realistic context of the goings-on of the culture at large. Both visions can be lived out in adulthood, depending on what path is chosen and acted out:

> I think being homeschooled is a good preparation for life. It's life. It's a continuation— being a child and then moving into adulthood— without the barriers that are put up by the compulsory education system. ... The coming of age, I think is a nice thing—to say you're done with this grade and now you're moving on to the next grade. I think in some ways it can be very empowering or a nice segue into adulthood, but unfortunately, I don't think our education system

does it very well. It focuses more on policing children and putting them in "boxes" rather than enlightening them, so I think homeschooling is much more enlightening and a much better preparation for going on to life.

From a child, [my son] was comfortable interacting with old people, babies, and everything in between, and that's pretty much how life is. Communication skills, interpersonal relationship skills, is in general what I think prepares someone to be a productive, happy, and healthy adult. It's a skill, I think, to learn how to go down a path to get what you want. To recognize your goal and then to set a pathway to follow to reach your goal, and I'm not sure that homeschooling does it differently, but I would suspect that homeschoolers do it a whole lot differently than people in school. Better. With more individual freedom, more of the ability to choose and not have things chosen for you so much.

When they're younger, I think kids should *not* be so pressured to choose and should be able to play more. Then in that play, and in those skills they acquire playing with other kids and being around all ages—adults, babies, and elderly, as homeschoolers do—I think they have a better feel for what they want to do, hopefully, and be able to spot what they want to do and all that. So that when they get older—as teenagers or whatever— then they can begin working toward those goals better than if they hadn't had a chance to play and develop all those communication skills with children.—*Pam, mother of one homeschooler and one grown former homeschooler, Durham, NC*

Competition and Success

Homeschooling by its very nature leaves room for a different and perhaps broader vision of success than the traditional monetary view of success. It is not necessarily defined by competition and achievement in the conventional sense (success based on rewards or grades and later salary). At the same time, homeschooling also affords lots of opportunity (as discussed earlier) for excellent preparation for traditional forms of success as well. Two homeschooling mothers talk about the kind of success they want their children to have:

> I think [kids] probably need to find ways to be more cooperative, not competitive. I think that's what school does, too—it teaches kids to be more competitive. It's all about what I got versus what you got. I know [my son] has this tendency to be competitive anyway, so my tendency is to help him to not be competitive but to find ways to work together with other people to make a better result. Make it more fun. I don't think competitiveness is something you need to teach kids; it's probably better to steer away from it. I think what happens is that it ends up being a lose-lose situation when you get into [constant] competition.—*Missy, homeschooling mother of two, Cary, NC*

> In my own public school experience, I felt I was only a cog in the machine of public education and that my particular gifts and talents were of no value. The goal was to get all A's so that you could attend the most prestigious college. At college the goal was, once again, to get all A's so you could make the most money. Those are not the "goals" I have in mind for my children. I am not interested in them pursuing academics solely for the purpose of making the best salary possible. I want them to discover what they were made to do—how they can use their gifts and talents to make a difference in our world. I will not judge the "success" of the "education" based on their

salary at graduation.—*Amy, homeschooling mother of three, upstate New York*

When different parents have different views on what success and the real world are, it is easy to see why they would make different choices to help prepare their children for these goals. Those who want something different for their children than the conventional monetary success understandably choose a different path than the conventional path to reach that success. Still, the evidence indicates that whatever their goal, homeschoolers excel in the "real" adult world. They grow up witnessing it, interacting with it, and participating in it. When they reach adulthood, they find themselves quite familiar and comfortable with it.

Homeschoolers have a similar experience with another closely related aspect of adulthood and growing up: learning good citizenship, which will be explored in depth in the next chapter.

chapter twelve

CITIZENSHIP AND DEMOCRACY

"Progress lies not in enhancing what is, but in advancing toward what will be."—Kahlil Gibran

"I am equally convinced that no program of social and political change that does not include and begin with changes in the ways in which we bear and rear children has any chance of making things better."—
John Holt, Teach Your Own

Parallel to the question of preparation for the real world is the question of citizenship. How will children learn good citizenship without going to school? Are homeschooled children insulated or sheltered from pluralism and democracy? What will happen to the citizenry if so many children are homeschooled?

These are concerns regularly expressed about homeschooling, and interestingly so. But research and experience suggest that homeschooled children are in a unique position to develop positive senses of citizenship and pluralism simply by being homeschooled.

What Is Good Citizenship?

The question of whether homeschoolers learn good citizenship requires that we consider what good citizenship is. Is it looking out for the interests of other individuals and the community or society at large? Participating actively in shaping the community's future? Voting? Abiding by the law? Questioning political processes? Something else?

What is a citizen anyway? It is such a vague concept. What we all really are in is relationships with many individuals and groups. We are neighbors, friends, church members, volunteers, spouses, partners, colleagues, coworkers, caregivers, patrons, customers, business owners, teachers, [and the list goes on]. What makes us behave in a responsible and caring way in all these roles is that we believe our relationship to all these' people matters to the well-being of our world. What is hurting our nation is the carelessness of anonymity and unrelatedness. We are not committed to our fellow human beings. We are in the frenzied pursuit of our short-term goals. On any day of the week I will take a good sibling relationship over a large, impersonal, competitive, pop-culture-driven environment as a foundation for future relationships. ... Close ties in a healthy family nurture an individual for a lifetime and make us stronger. This also explains why homeschooled kids introduce themselves and exchange phone numbers ... [and] the obvious social skill apparent in a child that can take responsibility for forming friendships.—*Janice, homeschooling mother of two, Durham, NC*

Some would express good citizenship by questioning and striving to understand and improve the culture they live in. David, a nineteen-year-old who was

184

homeschooled his whole life, explains his reasons for choosing to go to college:

> The main reason I give in my [application] essay is because I feel sort of like I live in a world that's governed by all these ideas, and I don't really know where they came from or why they have come to be the dominant ideas in our society and so on. I wish I understood that to a greater extent, because there are a lot of things about the world that I feel ought to be different, but I don't necessarily know how they should be done instead of the way they are done. And I think that by learning why—you know, you get to learn about the ideas that have been—that really influence our lives today whether we realize that or not.—*David, nineteen-year-old, homeschooled since birth, Durham, NC*

The Reality of Homeschooling

Pragmatically, homeschoolers spend their days out in the world interacting with a variety of people, businesses, and so forth rather than "tracked" in classrooms grouped by age and ability. Because of the freedom the homeschooling schedule allows, homeschoolers and their families have great freedom to be involved in their communities as well as to travel and see many parts of the country and world if they so choose. There is no evidence that homeschoolers grow up with any sort of limited perspective on democracy or a pluralistic society, just as there is no evidence that public, private, or charter schools are producing superior citizens.

David, the nineteen-year-old from above, shares his opinion on the matter:

> You know, there [could be] cases in which somebody who is educated at home could

certainly—you know, their parents' intent is to protect them from evil ideas and raise them to think specific things. ... But I wasn't raised that way. I've always had plenty of opportunities to encounter—you know, to at least learn that other things are out there.

You listen to the radio, you read books, and I always knew that different people thought different things and different people looked like different things and behaved differently. I always knew that there were other countries and other cultures and so on, because people talk about that sort of thing all the time.—*David, nineteen-year-old, homeschooled since birth, Durham, NC*

In fact, homeschooling parents as a group tend to model active citizenship. Research has shown that homeschooling parents are significantly more likely than other parents to vote; financially support political causes; contact their elected officials about issues; participate in public meetings, events, and rallies; do volunteer work in the community; and participate in volunteer and community organizations (Lines 2001; Lines 2000; NHERI, "Fact Sheet IIIc" 2001).

Homeschooled children often participate in these activities. When the first chapter of the National Black Home Educators Resource Association was formed in 2001, its families gathered at the Capitol House and, says Eric Burges on the organization's Web site, "some of the legislators didn't know whose hand to shake first—so many 'little' hands were being extended to them" (Burges 2003).

Laurie, a homeschooling mother of two teens from Katonah, NY, explains how homeschooling facilitates learning about citizenship:

In homeschooling it is a whole different way of learning together, and people care about each other and care about issues. We have flexibility in our academics. I'm an activist, and we spend a lot of time on activist activities. That has been a lot of our focus. And I think that's what they mean when they say they feel more prepared: they've experienced so many things.—*Laurie, homeschooling mother of two, Katonah, NY*

But Don't Homeschool Parents Shirk Responsibility to the Community?

Some have suggested that homeschoolers are irresponsible to their community, "abandoning" the schools when they are the motivated parents who could do the most to help them. But can we really say that parents are shirking responsibility by standing up despite cultural pressure and doing what they feel is right for their kids? Can we really say that these parents would be better citizens if they chose what they believe to be the inferior method for their families of educating, socializing, and, in short, raising their kids in the name of responsibility to the community? Fortunately, this is not the nature of the choice, since many homeschooling parents believe they are making the right choice for both their own families and their communities at large. A community is composed of its citizens, so what is good for the children is ultimately good for the community as well.

Patricia M. Lines of the US Department of Education says that homeschooling families "have not turned their backs on the broader social contract as understood at the time of the Founding [of the United States of America]. Like the Antifederalists, these homeschoolers are asserting their historic individual rights so that they may form more meaningful bonds with family and community. In doing so, they are not abdicating from the American agreement. To the contrary, they are affirming it" (Lines 2000).

In fact, homeschoolers can be seen as doing a service to the public schools. Schools are a tax-supported public service originally intended to provide an equal education to every child who could not afford to get it elsewhere. Homeschoolers pay the same taxes as everyone else but do not receive tax funding, thus saving taxpayers millions of dollars (NHERI 2003; NHERI 2000). In fact, every child who is homeschooled opens up a free seat in a school classroom to a child who really needs the services of that school, at no expense to taxpayers or the schools and government. For every thirty or so homeschooled children, it is as if a new teacher has been hired to the public schools for free (but in actuality the funding comes from the pockets of these homeschoolers, who are waiving their right as taxpayers to receive free public education for their children). It would be as logical to say that childless couples shirk their responsibility to the schools and community by not having children.

Parents demonstrate, model, and teach good citizenship when they exercise their rights to do what they believe is best for their children and their community. Homeschooling parents demonstrate to their kids every day just by continuing to homeschool that it is important to do what they believe is right, regardless of whether the choice is popular. What could be more responsible to the community than to raise well-educated children and teach them to do what they believe is right, whether it is popular or not?

Homeschooling Encourages Conscientious Citizenship

Homeschooled children, who are questioned frequently by relatives, friends, acquaintances, and strangers alike, are on the whole well aware that they are living a life off the beaten path. As a result, they know there is more than one way of doing things and that cultural impressions and stereotypes aren't always correct. They generally want their family's "minority" approach and freedom of choice in education to be respected and protected. This can naturally carry over to promote understanding of other minority choices and differences.

Moreover, by a certain age, homeschooled children for the most part are aware of the legislation that affects their family's educational choices, as well as what this legislation means, how it came into being, and how it can be changed or protected. Since homeschooling families must remain informed about the legal status of homeschooling, and are often involved in related activism (Lines 2000), it is almost inevitable that homeschooled children witness first-hand how citizens are affected by, and involved in, lawmaking and democracy. Ultimately, though, parents who are good citizens will raise kids who are good citizens regardless of where they go to school.

Homeschooling Builds Community

Many families have also made the observation that homeschooling somehow encourages a sense of community. Spending time with kids and adults of all ages within an environment of friendship, support, and cooperation (homeschool families collaborate and pool resources but do not typically compete with each other for grades) rather than an environment of social and academic competitiveness helps many homeschooled kids to grow up with a sense of community that remains with them their entire lives.

Montie, a homeschooling mother of one teenager, tells of her experience with this:

> The very first day that we went to our homeschool support group meeting, [my daughter] was welcomed, as was I, as one of the members. We were not set aside, we were not singled out, everyone spoke to us, everyone was kind to us, and we were welcomed right into the group, whereas in public school I always felt there were cliques among the children and also among the parents. If you were not a member of that group— if you were new to the community—then you had to sort of struggle your way in or fight your way in to the different groups. I haven't felt that way at all in any homeschooling activity that we've been in—in any class, any support group, or any meeting of the parents. We have not experienced any cliquishness.

> ("There are some who have been friends for a long time, and they know each other better, but they aren't cliquey," adds her daughter.)

> That's true of the parents, too, but they don't exclude the person who's new; they actually make an effort to bring the new people in and get them acclimated—they want you to feel part of that group.

> All the parents at this homeschool group (we take turns teaching) are very respectful to all the children, they call them all by name, they speak to them all in a very nice manner, never condescending, never a loud voice, they're always very, very kind. The parents are very respectful toward each other. We help each other out if somebody is ill or somebody has surgery or

something; we're there picking up their kids or bringing them food, whatever needs to be done. I think the kids see that as an example of how to treat someone else. And *they're* treated with respect. I don't think they would hesitate to go up to any parent in the group and say, "I need this," or, "I'm having a problem," because they know that that parent would care enough about them. To me it's example—how the parents behave. But that's just my perception.

As far as the parents go, too—you don't even have to ask somebody, they know if you're going through a problem. They will call and ask, "What can I do for you?"

It's almost like a family in a way—a loosely knit family—where you become one of them and they take you in. I think homeschooling encourages community somehow. The particular group we're in always participates in some kind of service project several times a year and encourages that. Some of the families individually do service projects, like participating in Meals on Wheels or food bank or things like that within their own families as part of their curriculum—one of their classes, if you will, is to do community service.

And we've got people from all walks of life. Our group is very diverse: One of the fathers is a veterinarian, [another is] a computer engineer, we have two podiatrists, one man who owns a landscaping business, and we have a couple in computers. It's a fairly diverse group economically, and we have people who have one child all the way up to five children. [There are] different religious backgrounds, but everybody seems to get along, which is very unusual, I think—people from all those different walks of life to mesh together like that as well as they do. [It's the] common bond of homeschooling and their dedication to homeschooling. Common values as far as child-rearing—that's the commonality, though there are a lot of differences.—*Montie, homeschooling mother of one, Alamance County, NC*

Yes, it is true. Despite popular image, homeschooling helps children gain a sense of citizenship and community that becomes and remains part of their being throughout their lives. It is yet another way in which family unity and real world experience make socialization one of the great advantages of homeschooling.

chapter thirteen

TEENAGERS, IDENTITY, AND SENSE OF SELF

"He who knows others is wise.
He who knows himself is enlightened."
—*Lao Tsu*, Tao Te Ching

"If you just set out to be liked, you would be prepared
to compromise on anything at any time, and you
would achieve nothing."—*Margaret Thatcher*

"Success is liking yourself, liking what you do, and
liking how you do it."—*Maya Angelou*

Perhaps the place where the positive effects of homeschool socialization can be seen the most is in the teens. Listening to the experiences of homeschooled teens and their parents reveals clearly that homeschooling helps teens to develop a strong, healthy sense of self and independence that they will carry with them for years to come.

Homeschooling parents and teens comment repeatedly on this phenomenon:

[Some things I have noticed since we started homeschooling are] they are more independent, more responsible as they are more involved with younger siblings and household chores, comfortable with all ages including adults, and they have a better sense of self due to decreased peer pressure. When people have commented on how most teens are only comfortable with their peer group but my teens are very comfortable conversing with adults, they usually attribute this to the fact that they are homeschooled.

[They also get a strong] sense of family, a real closeness between siblings. They don't experience peer pressure like they would in school. They can be their own person, ... being able to set up a schedule that works for the child (for instance, starting school late morning for a child who is a night owl). Flexibility to take advantage of learning experiences as they come up. My teens were able to go on a missions trip in February [2006] to Trinidad. In early December we [went] with my husband on his business trip to Mexico.

We didn't find the school experience enjoyable for the most part. It was also very stressful for the kids. The system does not treat the kids as individuals, and not all the kids are the same. That's why I love homeschooling. —*Glenda, homeschooling mother of six, Ontario, Canada*

As far as their "identity" or sense of self, I think that [homeschooling] has had a positive effect. The children now like homeschooling, and the kids at school seem very accepting, some even envious, of them. They are doing something "different from the crowd" but still have friends that are public schooled. The teachers that my kids have had have been very positive, also. I think that this teaches a valuable lesson that it's okay to do what you need to do, not what the "mainstream" does.—*Lauriann, homeschooling mother of three, Las Vegas, NV*

Here is what some teens have to say about homeschooling and their senses of self:

[Homeschooling] was my choice; they allowed it. I wasn't feeling like I was fitting in with—well, the girls, particularly, because fashion and boys and thinking about who they wanted to be asked to go to the dance with and all that. I didn't give a [expletive deleted] about all that, to be frank. I felt it was folly to be concerned with such things.

I had felt alienated and just not comfortable. ...I ended up missing a lot of days. I finished up fourth grade, and then we had a small private school to see if being at home was really what we wanted to do. It was, so then we decided to just homeschool with another girl. That's what we're doing now. There was a boy who came in about halfway through the year, but we're no longer homeschooling with him.

[I think an ideal social environment for me to be in would be] kids, boy or girl, with similar interests. I feel like in this group here at the writing class—I feel pretty well accepted. [Two of my friends] play video games, skateboard, have seen "Gladiator"—that's one of the things I like about them. [Others] are pretty accepting. I thought in Friday School [a homeschool co-op] some of the kids and some of the teachers and parents got worried about some of the subject matter, some of the subjects that I am interested in, so I felt I had to tone it down, which I don't always like but know that that's something you have to do no matter what environment you're in. Tone down some of the stuff I talk about, some of my references. It's a good thing in some ways

195

because it's a life skill, but in other ways it makes you feel uncomfortable.

I consider it important to be thought of as intelligent and cunning. I like to be seen as well-spoken, and I don't like to present myself as one of the crowd. I don't think that's being true to myself, because I'm not one of the crowd (a sheep, if you will). I consider myself to be me.

[As far as feeling pressure to be something I'm not], I think that happens to most people, pretty much all people. But I don't let it get to me. I just think, "Well, it's me. They can take it or leave it."—*Rachel, thirteen-year-old homeschooler, Durham, NC*

I think when you're at school you're labeled and stuck in a group whether you feel like you're in that group or not. ... just because you dress similar or you talk similar or you look similar. I have a lot of friends who go to school from summer camps, dance classes, drama classes, or anywhere.

People really don't get [homeschooling]. People ask me, "You need to spend more time with your peers, right?" And it's like, "Who's your peers?" I think that peers are who you have similar interests with, not someone who's your own age. I spend time with other writers or other singers. Even though they may be twenty years older than me, they're my peers because we believe in similar things and like similar things. It's not like you're stuck in school with a room full of kids who may have nothing in common except for you're the same age.

When I was with these guys going to Wednesday school, some kids came out in their designer jeans and their designer belly-button-showing shirts, and they were talking about this store in this mall and this guy they saw, and I thought, "Wow, that's completely different from who I am." And in a school, they might not end up being popular because there might be someone who was more popular than them, but as an American, they're more "normal" than I am. For me, I'm very glad that I'm not "normal." I'm fighting against that system of what a teenage girl today should look like. When I get to St. Louis, I'm going to be pretty much decorating my room, and making more collages and plastering my room with collages—they're like bits of me. Then you can open the door and say, "Wow! This is Alicia."

[I never have the urge to go to high school.] Sometimes I feel like some of the things there would be nice to have, but for me they're not strong enough to get rid of all of the things that I don't like about school. If I started going to school, I'd definitely get a label put on me. Like I'd try to sit down somewhere maybe at lunch, and they'd say, "You can't sit here." I personally don't think I fit in any label, but I'd be put in one, I know. I'd hate it.

I spend a lot of good time with my mom, and recently I've been trying to be the same around everyone, so then it's easier to be closer to my mom or to agree that we disagree or stuff like that. Definitely I appreciate [being around my family more], and it's definitely not a pain. I know my parents now, so I don't necessarily agree with everything I know about them. We have different opinions; we're different people. I'm still glad that I know them. I know some people who go to school who don't really know their parents other than what their parents might think—don't know their past. It's almost like they're sticks, like it's not real. You just have parents, and they're "Mommy" and "Daddy" and you love them, like when you were little. But it needs to be deeper than that.

Everyone should love their parents. I do, and it's not a bad thing—it's definitely a good thing. But though I love them, sometimes I do not like what they do. And it's good to accept that. For a long time when I was little, mommy was just mommy. Of course she was going to be there, and of course she would, you know, give me a sandwich for lunch. But now mommy is more than just gonna give me a sandwich for lunch—I've got to make it myself. But aside from that, I'll talk to her about things and tell her things.—*Alicia, fifteen-year-old homeschooler, Durham, NC*

I have a lot of freedom. I don't have to think what a school's telling me to think. I probably spend more time with adults than kids my age. [I spend time with] kids my age not as much as other ages. Coin Club in West Palm Beach meets every two weeks; that's one of my favorite activities. [That's composed of] adults, mainly senior citizens. They all look up to me, in fact. I'm the one who's always winning the awards for my exhibits and articles and things. And scholarships.

Freedom of thought is really the one benefit I keep coming back to. To me, that's the main thing that makes me glad I'm homeschooled, because I don't want to have to think what everybody else does. I want to be able to have what I want to think and what I feel is the right thing. Free opinion. We don't follow a set plan, I don't have peer pressure of any kind—[including] regarding religion. ...That's one major part of my life that I feel I've benefited from a lot: lack of peer pressure and the freedom to think about religion.—*Francis, thirteen-year-old homeschooler, Boynton Beach, FL*

Homeschooled teens, as a group, seem very comfortable with themselves. And, perhaps for this reason, they seem to accept each other more, too. Homeschoolers of all ages comment that they feel accepted and experience less peer pressure than they did in school:

> For fun I like to play outside, and I like to play music—jazz. I play the piano. I like to play with my puppy. And I like to play on the computer, and sometimes I like to watch TV. With my friends we usually do girl stuff and gossip. Jewelry and talk about boys and stuff like that.

> It seems like in homeschooling there's less peer pressure. They won't pressure you into doing something. In public school they were like, "Oh, do you want to go do this?" and I'd be like, "No." And they'd be like, "Oh, come on," and you finally have to get a teacher involved, and even then the teacher might not do anything about it. That hasn't happened yet in homeschool.—*Kaitlyn, twelve-year-old homeschooler, Alamance County, NC*

Still, people often wonder whether teens enjoy homeschooling or are lonely. There do seem to be fewer teens in the homeschooling community than younger kids, and many homeschooled teens do wish there were more available peers. Therefore, many consider school. Some choose it. For others, homeschooling wins out. The deciding factor? Freedom.

One of the joys of homeschooling is that you can always adapt to the needs of the child. If a child reaches teen age and wants to try school, this is an option. If they prefer the freedom of homeschooling, that's an option, too.

Ten years ago, when today's teens were just becoming school age and perhaps starting out as homeschoolers, homeschooling was not as "big" as it is now. It is natural that there are fewer teen homeschoolers today than younger homeschoolers, of which there are many. The hordes of young homeschoolers who are bringing homeschooling to record numbers today may not experience this concern when they are teens. At that time, it may no longer be an issue at all. They may find themselves surrounded by a wide variety of teenaged friends whom they already know today, as they grow into adolescence together.

Why Some Teens Choose to Go to School

Today, though, teens do often feel a desire to be around more similar-aged people. For this and other reasons, many homeschooled teens choose to go to school at this age.

Marianne, homeschooling mother of one thirteen-year-old in Boynton Beach, Florida, says:

> My son has interest in going to high school and has applied. I always thought he would homeschool till college, but he insists that he wants to try it, so I said, "Okay, we'll try it and see how it works out." He seems to want to have more structure than we have now.—*Marianne, homeschooling mother of one, Boynton Beach, FL*

Her son adds his perspective:

> I just want to get into a good college. I want to be in the baccalaureate program; it's more recognition.—*Francis, thirteen-year-old home-schooler, Boynton Beach, FL*

Why Some Teens Prefer Homeschooling

On the other hand, many homeschooled teens who consider "trying" or returning to conventional school end up deciding to remain homeschooled. And some never have the urge to go to school at all. Here is what some of them have to say:

Of course, high school always crossed my mind. I did wish around ninth grade that there had been more people around; that did become a little frustrating. I did consider high school, but I guess when I weighed the pros and cons, homeschooling won out. I liked my freedom and the unstructured way of life I was used to. I had friends, especially who I saw on weekends, friends in the community and friends who go to school. Even though I am not around a big group of friends all the time and going to parties all the time and stuff, the friends I have I know I'll have forever, because I got to spend more time building [those friendships] and getting to know them. My mom doesn't even talk to her friends from high school anymore; they're more like acquaintances, not close friends. The relationships I've had growing up are real relationships I'll have my entire life, because I've *had* them my entire life.

I did go one day with a friend [to high school] to see what it was like. The thing I always loved so much about homeschooling is that if you got interested in something, you could always spend a good chunk of time on it. Even if you took a class or did a group activity about something with others, when the time was up, if you were still engrossed you didn't have to be done—you could keep going. What I found in that one day of high school, and now I'm finding the same thing in college, is that the bell rings, the kids have been watching the clock and waiting for class to end, and you have to stop. It's done. I found that really frustrating. Some subjects I found interesting, and then it would be time to stop. You don't even have time to get into it at all. And the kids seemed so bored.

I am not a very shy person, so I don't feel I have ever had trouble making friends. I did feel when I got into the teenage years there was a shortage of other kids my age around. Even so, I feel like I have better social skills than my school friends; I can talk to anyone. I'm not afraid to have a friend much older than me or to have a friend who's four years old. Of course, I also like to have friends my age. But age doesn't always matter. A lot of my school friends only know how to be around people their same age and only socialize with their peers. My life is just more integrated than that, I guess.

I've never been interested in smoking and drinking—I hate it, actually. A lot of parties and camps you go to, the teens end up smoking and drinking, and it's so superficial and fake that I don't feel like I missed *anything*. I went to a homeschool camp called Not Back to School Camp, and after that camp my social life skyrocketed. It was such a loving community. It was a special atmosphere where I met so many awesome people, and they're just really amazing support systems for me.—*Stephanie, eighteen-year-old college student, homeschooled until college, Katonah, NY*

I like homeschooling. I am applying to a school, and the only reason I'm doing that is because it's a snowboarding school. It's three months, and I want the opportunity to be coached in snowboarding and to live in the mountains.

I don't have the desire to go to high school—not after seeing it—because the classes are like forty-five minutes long. If I want to do math at home I do it for like an hour and a half, and I accomplish more one on one than in a large group. Also, the kids don't really want to learn and just wait for class to be over. No, I just haven't had the urge to go to regular high school.—*Julian, fifteen-year-old homeschooler, Katonah, NY*

Adjusting to High School After Homeschooling

When homeschooled teens do choose to go to high school, there is no evidence that they have any difficulty making this transition. Elizabeth, a homeschooling mother of three from Ontario, Canada, shares her observations on her son's shift to conventional high school:

Although he is a fairly reserved young man, he settled in very well and was liked by both the teachers and the other students. He assisted the other students with math and science when they experienced difficulties, and his wry sense of humour was a source of mirth, especially for the teachers. This year his teachers continue to be delighted with his work and his attitude, advising that they consider him to be a role model for the other students. Again, he is a year younger than most of the students in his classes. He likes his teachers; he finds the bright, hard-working kids to hang around. Most of his peers went off to university this year, so he is making friends with a new group. He plays chess with one friend, goes to Cadets with another, and plays badminton with a third. He has a wonderful relationship with his piano teacher, who sometimes takes him to

Toronto for concerts. He also gets along well with the (generally) older reservists with whom he plays in the pipe and drum band; if I cannot drive him somewhere, someone is always willing to pitch in and help out; he is considered to be hardworking and is well liked within the band.

He is well adjusted, a little shy, but his school would like to nominate him for a future leaders' type conference in Europe or the US this summer, with a series of UN-style debates, and he is seriously considering accepting their nomination.

I think he would have done okay academically remaining at home for high school, but I do think that the experience of having a variety of teachers and having to get along with students, not all of whom he liked, was very positive for him.—*Elizabeth, homeschooling mother of three, Ontario, Canada*

Adjusting to College and "Real Life"

Those who remain homeschooled through high school can have similarly smooth transitions to college and adult life. David, a nineteen-year-old quoted in an earlier chapter, explains what he is doing with the time between homeschooling and college:

Presently I'm still living at home, traveling occasionally, working, and taking miscellaneous classes at community college. Right now I'm doing part-time, sometimes full-time, construction work for somebody I know who has a construction company. [Before that] I worked at Duke for a while doing computer support. I am actually [also] working on my college applications.

I've always enjoyed music—playing music and listening to music, so that's one of my interests. I play viola, and I'd like to learn some other instruments as well. ... I was always more interested in pop music in various forms. And I've always liked reading and writing. I read novels quite frequently. I enjoy technological gadgets, so that's another one of my interests. I mess around with computers, and I have old computer equipment lying around. Most recently I've been working as a carpenter, so I have some of that. It's interesting. People like to hear, "I went to school and did this, these were my classes, and this was the subject I liked. Then I went to college and studied this, and that's who I am," but I think they're really deceiving themselves. It's not easy for a person to say who they are. But if they go through a program like that it's easier for them to sort of explain themselves to other people in a superficial way.—*David, nineteen years old, homeschooled all his life, Durham, NC*

Homeschooled teens often seem to have a uniquely firm handle on where they are going or want to go. They realize that they have many options: high school, college, the work force, and other, more creative options. They generally seem well prepared for the paths they select. And this, ultimately, may be what we would all hope for our children: the ability to succeed in whatever setting they choose. This, as time will show, may well be the true legacy of homeschooling.

chapter fourteen

THE HOMESCHOOLING PARENT'S SOCIAL LIFE

"More time, less o'clock."—Nancy Hundal, Camping

We have explored and discussed many aspects of homeschooled children's socialization and drawn whatever conclusions we are going to draw about it, but one important question remains unaddressed. Ultimately, it is not only the *children's* social lives that matter in the life of a family, but the parents' social lives as well.

Many potential homeschooling parents worry that they will be "cooped up" at home, with no coworkers and no time away from their kids. This is indeed a very important concern, because there is no doubt that it is important for parents, like kids, to have a healthy, full social life. It is widely considered a truth—and one almost any parenting book or family counselor will echo—that a parent cannot give a child what she needs if the parent himself is needy (for example, in desperate need of social contact or "self" time). Fortunately, homeschooling can be quite conducive to a satisfying grown-up social life. In fact, many parents find that while homeschooling successfully, both they and their kids enjoy a richer and more fulfilling social life than ever before.

Freedom, Revisited

As discussed earlier, people commonly worry that homeschoolers are "stuck at home," but this is rarely the case. Because school children, and even to a certain extent teachers, are stuck in school each day, literally forbidden to leave, it is easy to imagine that homeschoolers, who are perceived as doing their learning at home rather than at school, must be "stuck" at home each day. But this is not the case. On the contrary, homeschooling parents, like their kids, live their days "out in the world," coming and going as they please, often spending as much or more time out as they do at home. Rather than being somehow confined to the home, they have *chosen* to live the homeschooling life; they are free to go out at will, and they do. There is nothing to stop a family from venturing out to spend the day, part of the day, or more than a day visiting friends or relatives or going to museums, the beach, the park, the yard, the library, on trips, and so on. Homeschooling parents, like their kids, find that they have a great deal of freedom.

At the same time, when they *are* at home (or those who do choose to stay at home much of the time), they do so because they choose to. After all, it is only possible to be "stuck" somewhere that one can't leave when one wants to.

Some parents of very young children (for example, toddler or preschool age) do feel "tied down." However, many acknowledge that this is not so much a result of homeschooling as it is a result of parenting a young child. Like all children, homeschooled children become more independent as they grow older.

Missy, a homeschooling mother of an eleven-year-old and an infant, has this to say:

[I don't feel] stuck at home. I probably feel less stuck at home than my neighbor does because she has to be home at a certain time when her kids come home on the bus, whereas if I want to do something, we can just pick up and go as a family. And if it's a short thing, [my son] is old enough now that I can leave him at home now for half an hour or an hour to go and do something, so I don't feel stuck at home at all. I feel very mobile. And if we want to go on a trip as a family, we can go when there's not anybody else there.

When I go to the park, the homeschooling parents are there with their kids, so there's a lot of social interaction for me there. There are so many things the parents do that I feel like there is plenty of social interaction. Discussion nights, the ladies have gone out—there's plenty of opportunities to get out and do things socially, [even just] within the realm of homeschooling.

—*Missy, homeschooling mother of two, Cary, NC*

In fact, many homeschooling parents report that their social lives improve with homeschooling:

I think it's been positive for me because I, too, have made very good friends with some of the mothers. We live close enough together, and we have certain common bonds. I worked long hours prior to this and probably would not have socialized with the people who I worked with— not on a regular basis, anyway—partly because I was the supervisor and partly because of a lack of having things in common. So for me it's been positive. The only drawback I can see is that you don't have a lot of alone time, but my situation is that my husband works out of town a lot so I don't have someone to help me. But sending [my daughter] off to school and going to work, I didn't really have time alone anyway, come to think of it. But you just have to plan some time for yourself.

Homeschooling has been a very good decision for us. I'd certainly do it again and earlier if I could.—*Montie, homeschooling mother of one, Alamance County, NC*

Homeschooling has definitely affected my social life. Yeah, cause I know all these parents. I have more friends, people who I spend time to talk to. ... I feel much more connected to other people with children.—*Catherine, homeschooling mother of three, Durham, NC*

When a family is separated (for example, the kids are at school, the parents are at work), the parents typically must find friends outside of their kids' lives, and the kids must find friends apart from their parents' lives. The whole family runs in different "circles," each finding a separate group of friends and each having their own "life." In order to spend time with their friends, parents often must either do so apart from their children or "drag" the children along though their own friends are not there. (In some cases kids might bring friends along.) Likewise, in order for the children to spend time with their friends, they will often do so in the absence of their parents, who may not want to spend time with the friends or their friends' parents (or may not be welcome).

Conversely, if parents want to be with their kids, they may feel that they must do so at the expense of their own social lives with their own friends, at the expense of their kids' social lives with their friends, or both. (This may also lead to kids feeling like hanging out with their parents is boring, "lame," a nuisance, or a waste of time.) Because of this cultural pattern, it is easy to see why people imagine that homeschool parents and kids are isolated.

But this is really the result of a situation in which family members lead separate lives, only loosely connected to one another and only intersecting at certain points during the day or week. When parents and kids lead a unified life, spending their days together—as is often the case with homeschooling—they may actually enjoy a richer, fuller social life. Rather than having to limit their time with their friends in order to be with their families, homeschooling families are free to be with friends and family simultaneously by spending time with other families or groups of families. The children will often play with the other children while the parents socialize with the other parents. At the same time, the parents are present and available to the children, and the children are supervised by the parents. The adults, like the kids, have plenty of time and freedom to get to know one another quite well, not feeling such a need to cut short their time together in order to be with their families, because they are already with them.

Elizabeth, a homeschooling mother from Hillsborough, North Carolina, tells how her social life has changed with homeschooling:

> The way that we choose to do homeschooling means that I'm in a community of supportive parents. I suppose I would be in a community—I would think of school parents as a community of supportive parents, but we have much more overlap and more in common because we're with our kids, together parenting, for big chunks of days. And so there's support, information, modeling, and connection around being a parent and being a part of my family that I get from the other parents, which I think is much more the way human beings have been for the millennia than is typical these days.

One of the big things that we definitely observed is that once we had kids, and particularly when we started homeschooling and are on a homeschooling sort of schedule (which means that we are available as a family at different times than other families are), that our social life tended to be more with families and particularly with homeschooling families. So it's a smaller group of people, but it's a more intimate community. I think as a person I feel some lack of having friends who don't have children. For instance, you know there's a little less diversity in my pool, because if we're going to spend a chunk of time with somebody, then it needs to work for everybody at least marginally well. So I'm not as likely [to be with people who don't have kids]. The balance of that is growth in lots of areas that are related to being in a family: being a parent, being in a couple and a family. So it's just an exchange, and I'll get to do some of that other stuff at a different time. And I still work at carving out some of that as my kids get a little older. It feels like an exchange.

Part of my thinking was, "It might be kind of nice to have me and [my husband] go out with some of our friends sometime and have some time that was attending to each other in that kind of way, a cohort of adult friends hanging out, continuing to value those relationships." And I think that I feel a little bit of a sense of loss of that. But that isn't homeschooling, that's just being a parent and the way I choose to be a parent. But I think it's partly related, because an extension for me of homeschooling is that we value being together as a family and that we don't just hand off here and there. Our kids have not been with babysitters regularly, except for grandparents occasionally. I imagine there will be blocks of time that will appear because they are naturally what my kids are needing and doing where they'll go spend the night overnight with somebody or something like that, and we'll go, "Oh! Here we are. What shall we do? Maybe we could get together with some adults who don't have children or get together with some parents of our kids' friends or whatever." That already has changed a lot.—*Elizabeth, homeschooling mother of two, Hillsborough, NC*

I don't know if it's maybe just that we fit better with [the homeschoolers] than where we were headed to [before], but it's just like my comfort level with the people that are doing this and the kids and what they're being exposed to, it's so high compared to in the schooling situation.... Everybody I've met in [our homeschool group] is what I call "thoughtful." It is about making that homeschool choice that we talked about. This is not something that is self-evident. It's not on the plate of choices when you just blindly kind of go through society. If you just kind of live the way you're "supposed" to live—if I blindly follow that path—I will never come to homeschool. You'll put your kid in school, you'll force them to do the homework, you'll make them do well, as well as they can do.

If you blindly go down that path, you'll never see homeschooling as an option. So anyone who makes it to the homeschooling choice has by definition naturally backed up off that "I'm gonna do what I'm supposed to do and head down this path." And I'm gonna look at what my options are, and I'm gonna think about it, and I'm gonna decide which one is better for me. And a lot of people do that. I'm sure a lot of people have done that, and I'm sure they're staying with public school. But if they *have* done that, then they're part of a crew that now there are some of them that have actually made a choice. But there's a big population there that has just blindly gone that way. So people who have made it to homeschooling have certainly made that choice, certainly stepped back and made that thoughtful decision to do this option. I think that alone makes them all have something in common.

I've been able to come up with this choice that I think fits even though it wasn't mainstream, or it wasn't exactly the way it's supposed to go. I think that is just that fundamental thought—that gives them a commonality. But it's a commonality on something so basic as to say, "Look, I'm not going to just blindly go down a path because that's where society points me." It's such a basic commonality that it doesn't even have to be homeschooling. If you can find other people who have that same commonality with you, you'll be very comfortable with them and very friendly with them. It's just a very easy way to find them. I guarantee that this pool of homeschoolers, no matter what else I know about them, I know that they have this in common with me. And then there's, of course, tremendous differences that weed out who I'm gonna be friends with and who I'm not. ... If you look at [our homeschooling group], we probably run the gamut from one end of the spectrum just as much as any other group of people, so there are still the differences among us all, but we still have that one commonality: that fundamental thing that we're *deciding.—James, homeschooling father of three, Durham, NC*

Many parents report that they have plenty of freedom to pursue their own interests, concerns, and even careers while homeschooling, because they are available to their children while they do it.

Time for Self

And, strangely enough, many parents report that homeschooling does not detract from their time to themselves. While they are responsible for kids all day, they make their own schedules and may have good support from other friends in the homeschooling and general communities. Homeschoolers often "trade off" kids for periods of time, taking turns "watching" each other's kids either for play or for teaching and may barter with each other for time through childcare co-ops as well.

Carisa, a mother of four from Miami, Florida, compares her alone time while homeschooling to her alone time now that her kids are in school:

> I put my kids in school this year. I don't get it. I'm spending four or five hours a day now helping them with homework, which is exactly what I was doing when we were homeschooling. I literally do not have any more time for myself now than I had when we were homeschooling. This going to school thing is a lot harder than homeschooling. Don't ever give it up! We'll be back to homeschooling next year.—*Carisa, mother of four, Miami, FL*

And a number of homeschooling parents consider feeding their own minds a high priority while homeschooling. Sarah, mother of four lifelong homeschoolers, two of whom are now grown, says:

> I feel very strongly that once the child gets old enough to have any independence at all, the parent needs to have their own work—important work—that they are doing. It needs to be interruptible work, but important work.—*Sarah, mother of four, Durham, NC*

It seems that, just as homeschooling offers great rewards for kids socially, so, too, can it offer a rich, fulfilling social life to parents. The family-based, community, and real-world living that homeschooling so often embodies benefits all members of the family. Homeschooling does not have to be a land of sacrifice for parents. On the contrary, for many parents, it is a land of plenty.

chapter fifteen

SOCIALIZATION
AND SUCCESS

*"The one outstanding and impressive fact that did
leap from the pages was that
there was a strong and loving figure, usually a
mother, father, or other family
member, who spent time with that person during
their childhood. With some
notable [self-taught] exceptions ... it was a person,
not a school, that made a
difference in the lives of these famous and successful
people."—Mac and Nancy Plent,* An "A" in Life:
Famous Home Schoolers

*"The heresy of one age becomes the orthodoxy
of the next."—Helen Keller*

As discussed briefly in an earlier chapter,
homeschoolers as a group enjoy remarkable academic
success. Each year it becomes more and more clear that
homeschooling is a highly effective method in terms of
educating children. For example, many studies have
shown that homeschoolers consistently score

exceptionally well on standardized tests (Rudner 1999; Ray 1999), and that scores become higher the longer a child has been homeschooled (Ray 1997). In the US, homeschoolers have been described as "dominating" national contests, such as the national spelling and geography bees, and they are now sought after by many colleges and universities due to their excellent preparation for college success (Honawar 2002; Reynolds 2003; Jefferson 2000; Vernon, "Washington State Eighth Grader Wins National Geographic Bee" 2003; Vernon, "Ten Students Advance to Geographic Bee Finals" 2003; Danielson 2002). This success is evident regardless of which method a homeschooling family uses to educate their children.

Whatever the objections to homeschooling may be, there is no getting around the fact that homeschooling proves daily to be an exceptionally effective educational approach, which raises the following questions: "What makes homeschooling so effective academically? What is the deciding difference? In other words, what is it that sets homeschooling—in all its many forms—apart from conventional schooling?" Whatever it is will essentially define homeschooling and most likely be responsible for homeschooling's broad academic success.

Studies have also shown that homeschoolers excel across the board—parental education doesn't seem to matter, curriculum use (or non-use) doesn't seem to matter, and money spent doesn't seem to matter (Rudner 1999). Some homeschoolers follow strict curricula, some "unschool," some have families of one child and some of ten, some are conservative, some liberal, some rural, some urban, some rich, some poor (Bauman 2001; Bielick, et al 2001; Rudner 1999). Despite this wide range of differences, homeschoolers are amazingly consistent in their academic success.

Why? What is it that draws such a disparate group together demographically? Homeschoolers have a few key things in common: low child-to-adult ratio, very heavy parental involvement, and the homeschooling lifestyle—family-centered living and learning in the community. In other words, the one thing that unifies all homeschoolers is nothing other than homeschooling's unique *social environment*. It is these factors that account for the astounding and consistent academic success of all types of homeschoolers.

Put another way, the only unifying factor that really sets homeschoolers apart from traditional schoolers is this: they are homeschooling. They have parents who have made this choice, and rather than being in a classroom, they are with their families and out in their communities. They are living, learning, and socializing in the family and community, the very same things that define homeschool socialization.

Yes—the bottom line is that it is *socialization* itself that sets homeschooling apart and defines and distinguishes it from all other forms of schooling. Though socialization is often thought of as a drawback of homeschooling, and though many choose not to homeschool or not to support it due to socialization concerns, it may ironically be the case that socialization is the single most important factor in homeschooling, even scholastically. As homeschoolers demonstrate remarkable academic success, it just may be the unique social environment homeschoolers enjoy that makes homeschooling so effective.

Of course, it should come as no surprise that such things as family unity and real-world experience would encourage academic success. Educators and social scientists have long heralded close family ties and parental involvement as key elements in academic and future success (Levine 1998). Low ratio of child to adult, a situation intrinsic to the family context (even in the largest families), is also widely recognized to be an important factor in educational effectiveness. And a lack of peer pressure, bullying, and other social problems contributes to children's ability to learn and excel academically as well. (For example, bullying has been shown to have detrimental effects on academic performance, as discussed earlier.)

It is a simple fact that socialization (in the form of family socialization) is intimately and inextricably intertwined with academic success (Levine 1998).

In school, academics and social life influence each other immensely. It is widely acknowledged that social problems and pressures are associated with academic difficulties. In school, there may be social pressure to be smart, or there may be social pressure *not* to be smart. (It may be considered "uncool" and "nerdy" to be "too" smart or studious.) Children who try too hard, are too smart, or study too much risk being labeled "nerds;" those who are not smart enough may be considered "dumb" or "losers." In this way, the social system strongly encourages a norm of mediocrity. At the same time, paradoxically, students are often compared to or pitted against each other academically and are then suddenly assigned to work in groups where they are forced to depend on one another for their own academic success. Suddenly, it is temporarily cool to be smart (others may desire to be in your group), yet beneficial to be lazy (others may do the work for you).

Similarly, the relationship students must have with adults in a typical school setting is paradoxically adversarial yet dependent, and students are alternately encouraged and forbidden (depending on the situation) to request help from teachers and other students.

One homeschooling mother talks about homeschooling's benefits in regards to this:

> I've never really thought about what is the primary benefit [of homeschooling]. There are a lot of benefits. But I think they all build on that: that my children know who they are, what they know, how to find out more, and they're never afraid of showing ignorance. That it's okay to not know something. Well, "never" is a hard word. As a rule, they don't have any qualms about showing ignorance in something, because that's just another place to look for information if they want it, or to say, "No thanks, I don't want any information on that right now."—Sarah, mother of four, Durham, NC

Whereas social difficulties tend to interfere with academic achievement, conversely, family involvement is widely recognized to be a highly positive factor in successful learning. The things that make homeschooling successful are the same things that make some students successful in a school environment: parental involvement and concern, one-on-one attention, and the list goes on.

Beth Levine's *Reader's Digest* article "Help Your Child Excel in School: Tips From Top Teachers" states that to foster a love of learning, parents "have to show kids that learning doesn't stop with a grade or a diploma—it's a way of life." Levine quotes acclaimed teacher Gina Rau as saying, "I believe the most important thing is to spend time with your kids." It mentions, moreover, that research has shown that kids whose families eat together have higher literacy rates (Levine 1998). Although these tips are intended for teachers and parents in dealing with schoolchildren, they reflect the same principles that homeschooling is based on.

This is one reason (perhaps the main reason) that homeschooling is so successful academically, since parental involvement in the child's life and education is widely recognized to be a primary factor in children's scholastic success. (How ironic, then, that parents being "too involved" is a common fear outsiders have regarding homeschoolers' socialization, given that this very involvement is a large part of why homeschoolers do so well.) As Levine points out in her article, "Dozens of studies support the connection between a child's scholastic achievement and consistent parental interest and involvement—regardless of the parent's educational background" (Levine 1998).

Homeschoolers' success does not in any way negate the success of the many excellent school-going students who pursue and achieve a successful education in school. The reason homeschoolers achieve very highly *across the board* rather than just a small percentage of them doing so, as occurs in schools (this is known as a "bell curve"), is that homeschooling *embodies* and is defined by these very factors that are known to create quality education:

> [My son] spends time at home with us where we have animals to care for, and he can learn archery. [He does] some of these things that [our homeschool group] does, and he's also taking martial arts. I think as he grows older, in terms of more academic things, it'll be just more like an open study—independent study—earlier. Most of us didn't even begin to experience that until college. "Is it gonna be on the test?" That was the question. That was mantra of at least my childhood, and all of this emphasis on scoring big on the test. And I understand all that, and I certainly want him to get a good academic education—I'm not ignoring that, either. I just think there's a way of enterprising things a little differently. And also I'd like him to pursue knowledge, not just information. Hopefully that

will come about. I think that's a parent's job, and as a homeschooler you're taking on a much bigger dose of that. In my experience, most parents don't feel themselves capable of teaching their children. They figure that's a specialized job for a professional teacher; "I'm not one; they should do it." And I'm not degrading professional teachers, but teaching conditions—I did it, I know what the classroom is like. It's rough.

I think we're on the road to a good basic education with basic skills; I also want him to know how to pursue something that he's interested in, and I think he's had quite a special childhood so far, living where we do and all the opportunities he's had. I think most important are some good values and some self-confidence and an ability to know how to pursue what he wants to pursue. I was always told, "Do whatever you want to do, just do it the best you can." And I think by homeschooling you might inherently open more doors than the typical public school education. I think there are other things to consider beyond what is the "curriculum." I mean, the teacher's got twenty, thirty kids in each classroom. They can only give so much attention to each student, and with [my son], I think particularly as he grows older, he'll really be able to develop some skills and interests—he already has—and I think that's the most important thing, to keep self-motivated. I think that's the key to success: be interested in what you're doing and be able to motivate yourself. And I think in a good homeschool environment that can really grow.—*Steven, homeschooling father of one, Mebane, NC*

As I said before, I don't believe that any other person, no matter how skilled as a teacher, would know my child better than I do. I think this gives me a tremendous advantage, and I also believe

223

that most of what a young child needs to know he can learn for himself with only minimal assistance from me. In public school the "goal" is to get children reading as quickly as possible. But in our homeschool the goal is to develop a lifelong love of reading and learning in our children. Those two goals are VERY different. Our children have the freedom to explore the topics that are interesting to them, at the exact moment of their own choosing.

Because I knew my son better than anyone else, because he trusted me and I trusted him (our strong relationship that grew from spending the majority of our time together), he had the freedom to learn in the best way for HIM. My other son, at age five, is already interested in reading and is learning alongside his seven-year-old brother. Because of our relationships, I am able to discern what is the right approach for each of our individual children. And because I am not working in a public school setting, I have the freedom to work with each individually and to work according to their interests, not MY imposed schedule.

This relationship and trust also has the added benefit of helping my children discover their natural gifts and talents. In a public school the "goal" is to achieve as high an academic score as possible. In our homeschool the academic goal (and academics are not our first priority) is to discover what you love doing and to learn to do it well. I am not imposing my set of "required academics" upon my children and stifling their innate curiosity and gifts. I am watching and learning alongside them. I don't dictate what they learn, although I may need to offer some guidance occasionally.

Certainly I will instruct them to ensure that they have basic life skills, but that is not something I must strive to "instruct" them. They learn those skills by living alongside me (spending their days at home and not separated from me) and by learning to do what I do. My role would be better described as "learning companion" than "instructor." I can only take on this role if my child and I have a strong relationship and great trust in one another. If I don't trust my child, I will not believe that he can learn for himself and will be more likely to try to force instruction upon him. If my child doesn't trust me, he may either rebel against my "instruction" or forsake his natural gifts in the interest of becoming who he perceives I want him to be.—*Amy, homeschooling mother of three, upstate NY*

Family is the key

Whether a child is homeschooled, conventionally schooled, or otherwise, it is the *family* who is ultimately responsible for the child's education and socialization. It is in the family that the entire foundation for the child's future success and happiness is laid. Like the family, mass culture is made up of individual human beings. When we deal with society we can see it either as a cold, lonely mass of nameless, meaningless faces, or we can approach each person as an individual. When we walk into a company office to work, for example, it matters not whether we have ever set foot in a classroom full of children our own age, but whether we have the skills and compassion to do our jobs and to interact and resolve issues with other individuals with creativity, understanding, and integrity. Homeschooling offers children the opportunity to learn these skills through years of guidance and practice in living and resolving conflicts with people they love, care about, and must continue to live with every day for many years. And ultimately, both the skills and the relationships built in this manner will remain with the child into adulthood.

In fact, whatever our academic or career paths, successes, and levels of achievement, it is ultimately our personal relationships—with friends, coworkers, spouses, kids, and yes, parents and siblings—that determine and create our happiness throughout our lives. It is the skills we learn from living on a day-to-day basis with others whom we care about, and the relationships we build, that truly determine our future happiness.

Resources, Tips, and How-To

N ot much is needed in order to have a rewarding homeschool social life. General parenting skills are really the most important resource, and homeschooling helps develop these further. Beyond that, some resources are listed below that may be helpful to the family getting started or continuing with homeschooling.

Finding Other Homeschoolers

Within each state and province there are many smaller organizations, associations, support groups, e-mail networks, and playgroups. Your statewide organization may be able to direct you to some of these, and the Web sites listed below may also be helpful in finding a group:

Statewide organizations (United States)

Alabama

Home Educators of Alabama Round Table
alabamahomeschooling.com

Alaska

Alaska Private and Home Educators Association
www.aphea.org

Arizona

Arizona Families for Home Education
www.afhe.org

Home Education Network of Arizona
www.hena.us

Arkansas

Home Educators of Arkansas (HEAR)
www.geocities.com/Heartland/Garden/4555/
index.html

California

California Homeschool Network (CHN)
californiahomeschool.net/default.htm

Christian Home Educators Association of California
www.cheaofca.org

Homeschool Association of California
www.hsc.org

LDS Homeschooling in California
ldshomeschoolinginca.org

Colorado

Christian Home Educators of Colorado
www.chec.org

Concerned Parents of Colorado
members.aol.com/treonelain/

Connecticut

Connecticut Homeschool Network
www.CTHomeschoolNetwork.org

Delaware

Delaware Home Education Association
dheaonline.org

Florida

Florida Parent Educators Association
www.fpea.com

Home Education Foundation
www.flhef.org

LIFE of Florida
www.lifeofflorida.org

Georgia

Georgia Home Education Association
www.ghea.org

Home Education Information Resource
www.heir.org

Hawaii

Hawaiihomeschool
groups.yahoo.com/group/Hawaiihomeschool.

Christian Homeschoolers of Hawaii
www.christianhomeschoolersofhawaii.org

Satori Dharma Hawai'i
satoridharmahawaii.htmlplanet.com

Idaho

Christian Homeschoolers of Idaho State
www.chois.org

Idaho Coalition of Home Educators
www.iche-idaho.org

Illinois

Illinois H.O.U.S.E
www.illinoishouse.org

Indiana

Indiana Home Educators
www.ihen.org

Iowa

IDEA (Iowans Dedicated to Educational Alternatives)
Unschooling Support Group
www.avalon.net/~pdiltz/idea

Network of Iowa Christian Home Educators
www.the-niche.org

Kansas

Christian Home Educators Confederation of Kansas
www.kansashomeschool.org

Kentucky

Christian Home Educators of Kentucky
www.chek.org

Kentucky Home Education Association
www.khea.8k.com

Louisiana

CHEF of Louisiana
www.chefofla.org

Louisiana Home Education Network
www.la-home-education.com

Maine

Maine Home Education Association
www.geocities.com/mainehomeed

Maryland

Maryland Home Education Association
www.mhea.com

Maryland Association of Christian Home Educators
www.machemd.org

Massachussetts

Massachussetts Home Learning Association
www.mhla.org

Massachussetts Homeschool Organization of Parent
Educators
www.masshope.org

Michigan

Network of Michigan Home Educators
nmhe.tripod.com

Minnesota

Minnesota Association of Christian Home Educators
www.mache.org

Minnesota Homeschoolers Alliance
www.homeschoolers.org

Mississippi
Mississippi Home Educators Association
www.mhea.net

Missouri
Missouri Association of Teaching Christian Homes
www.match-inc.org

Montana
Montana Coalition of Home Educators
www.mtche.org

Nebraska
Nebraska Christian Home Educators Association
www.nchea.org

Western Nebraska Home Educators Network
www.geocities.com/western_nebraska

Nevada
Nevada Homeschool Network
www.nevadahomeschoolnetwork.com

New Hampshire
New Hampshire Homeschooling Coalition
www.nhhomeschooling.org

New Jersey
Alliance of Home Educators
www.geocities.com/ahe_nj

New Mexico
Christain Association of Parent Educators New
Mexico (CAPE-NM)
www.cape-nm.org

New York

APPLE Family and Homeschool Group

www.applenetwork.us/ny/apple.html

New York Home Educators' Network
www.nyhen.org

North Carolina

North Carolinians for Home Education (NCHE)
www.nche.com

Homeschool Alliance of North Carolina
www.ha-nc.org

North Carolina Unschoolers
www.ncunschoolers.com

North Carolina African-American Homeschoolers
ncaahomeschoolers.tripod.com

North Dakota

North Dakota Homeschool
groups.yahoo.com/group/northdakotahomeschool

Ohio

Christian Home Educators of Ohio
www.cheohome.org

Oklahoma

Eclectic Home Educators
eclectichomeeducators.faithweb.com
Home Educator's Resource Organization (HERO) of

Oklahoma
oklahomahomeschooling.org

Oklahoma Christian Home Educators Consociation
www.ochec.com

Oregon
Oregon Christian Home Education Association
Network
www.oceanetwork.org

Oregon Home Education Network
www.ohen.org

Latter-Day Saint Oregon Home Educators
Association
www.lds-ohea.org

Pennsylvania
Pennsylvania Home Educators Associatoin
www.phea.net
Pennsylvania Home Education Network
www.phen.org

Rhode Island
Parent Educators of Rhode Island
P.O. Box 782
Glendale, RI 02826
Rhode Island Guild of Home Teachers
www.rihomeschool.com

Secular in the Ocean State
www.soshomeskoolri.org

South Carolina
South Carolina Home Educators Association
www.schomeeducatorsassociation.org

South Dakota
Alternative Instruction Association of South Dakota
www.geocities.com/aia_cc

South Dakota Christian Home Educators
www.sdche.org

Tennessee
Tennessee Home Education Association
tnhea.org

TnHomeEd
www.tnhomeed.com

Texas
Texas Home School Coalition
www.thsc.org

Utah
Utah-homeschool-network
http://groups.yahoo.com/group/utah-homeschool-network
Utah-hs
http://groups.yahoo.com/group/Utah-hs/

Vermont
Vermont Association of Home Educators
www.vermonthomeschool.org

Virginia
Home Educators Association of Virginia
www.heav.org

The Organization of Virginia Homeschoolers
www.vahomeschoolers.org

Washington
Washington Homeschool Organization
www.washhomeschool.org

West Virginia

Christian Home Educators of West Virginia
www.chewv.org

West Virginia Home Educators Association
www.wvhea.org

Wisconsin

Wisconsin Christian Home Educators Association
www.wisconsinchea.com

Wisconsin Parents Association
www.homeschooling-wpa.org

Wyoming

Homeschoolers of Wyoming
www.homeschoolersofwy.org

Canada

Association of Canadian Home-Based Education
www.flora.org/homeschool-ca/achbe/index.html

Other places to look for homeschoolers

- Ask at your church, synagogue, or community center
- In a local breastfeeding or attachment parenting support group
- Post a notice at a health or natural foods store
- Call the local parks and recreation department or the state department of education
- If you see events or classes advertised in your community for homeschoolers, go to them. Sometimes local skating rinks, bowling alleys, libraries, bookstores, and so forth will have

"homeschool" sessions or events that you could attend and meet other homeschoolers.

Starting Your Own Group

If you have tried and can't seem to find a group or association in your area that meets your needs, then chances are you are not the only one looking. Consider starting your own group. This could be something as simple as a homeschool or pre-homeschool playgroup.

Try posting notices that say something like, "Looking for homeschoolers (or pre-homeschoolers) to form playgroup," or, "Local homeschooling group forming. If interested, call _____." If you are looking for a particular demographic of homeschooler or want to form a particular kind of group, you could specify that. (For example, you could indicate that you are looking for Christian homeschoolers, forming a secular homeschool group, hoping to form an inclusive group, or something along these lines.) Try posting these notices at your place of worship, local natural foods store, library, community center, and so on. Chances are good that if you are looking for other homeschoolers, they are looking for you, too.

Helpful books

Homeschooling for Excellence by David and Micki Colfax
Family Matters by David Guterson
A Sense of Self: Listening to Homeschooled Adolescent Girls by Susannah Sheffer
Dumbing Us Down by John Taylor Gatto
Homeschooling: Take a Deep Breath—You Can Do This! by Terrie Lynn Bittner
Punished by Rewards and *No Contest* by Alfie Kohn
The Teenage Liberation Handbook by Grace Llewellyn
Teach Your Own by John Holt

Children Are From Heaven by John Gray, Ph.D.
(see bibliography for more information)

Supportive magazines

Mothering
Life Learning
Home Education
Homeschooling Today

Helpful Web sites

www.learninfreedom.org
www.hslda.org
www.homeschooling.gomilpitas.com
www.homeschoolingstuff.com
www.nssc1.org
www.safechild.org
www.bullybeware.com
www.pta.org/programs
www.weprevent.org
www.bullying.co.uk
www.nobully.org.nz

Tips

1. If you are a new homeschooler, **be patient**. Homeschool groups do not have buildings with signs on them making them easy to find, but they are out there. If you look, you will find one. And once you find one, the people in it will probably be able to tell you about others as well.

There are different types of groups to meet the needs of different types of homeschoolers. For example, some religiously oriented groups require a faith statement and others don't; some groups are secular or "inclusive"; others are oriented toward a more specific demographic, such as Jewish homeschoolers, Christian homeschoolers, unschoolers, and so on. If the first group you find does not fit your needs, keep looking. Whatever your philosophy or criteria, there are others out there like you, and they may be looking for you as well.

2. Remember that, especially if your child has been in school, the "switch" to homeschooling is a transition. It takes time to adjust. You will probably experience some immediate benefits, but the overall transition requires patience. Children often need time to "decompress" from the school environment. This can take anywhere from a few weeks to a year (largely depending on how long the child has been in school). Being aware of this real need and respecting it will make your job and your child's transition much easier and more pleasant.

Sometimes this means allowing the child to "do nothing"—that is, be literally on vacation—for a while as they adjust to the new way of life. They are not *really* doing nothing, of course. They are completely restructuring their expectations; re-evaluating their trust relationships with their parents and others; adjusting to a new routine; and shifting to a new outlook on learning, their options, and even perhaps the world. This may be invisible to the outside world and may look like playing at the park or reading novels for hours in pajamas, but it is hard work and important work. It is the first major task of a new homeschooler, and they must do it one way or another before they can move on.

Since homeschooling is so efficient and effective, you will not lose time (in terms of "academic" learning) by respecting this decompression period. In fact, it will probably make learning much easier in the long-term.

How to get started

As discussed in this book, social interaction and learning come in many forms for homeschoolers, including playing with other kids, family time (talking to parents, playing with siblings, and so forth), and real-life interactions with other adults and children in the community.

There are many ways to accomplish these things. Some ways to get started include the following:

- Join a homeschool group.
- Find other homeschool friends outside of a group.
- Consider your day-to-day activities at home (for example, breakfast, lunch, chores, bedtime, and so forth) as important times that you are together. Be flexible; if a conversation comes up that your child wants to continue discussing with you, go with it. Your time belongs to you; schedules are tools for your use and needn't control your lives.
- Help siblings see each other's point of view.
- If something interests your child, support him in pursuing that interest in age-appropriate ways. Take him to the library and help him find books on the subject if he wants; sign her up for a class in the community with or without other homeschoolers if you see fit; offer to take them to meet someone interesting who knows more about the subject. But don't overdo it; let the children be the guide. If they lose interest, let it go. Just listen to them, and follow their lead.
- Do things together that your family enjoys. When you homeschool, your life is yours to live. Enjoy it! Your kids will learn to live a life they enjoy as well.

Good luck!

appendix b

FAMOUS AND IMPORTANT HOMESCHOOLERS THROUGHOUT HISTORY

Artists

Ansel Adams (Photographer)
Leonardo da Vinci
Claude Monet
John Singleton Copley
Andrew Wyeth
Jamie Wyeth

Performing artists

Charlie Chaplin
Frankie Muniz
Hanson (Sibling singing group)
Jennifer Love Hewitt
LeAnne Rimes
Louis Armstrong
Moffatts (Canadian version of Hanson)
Whoopi Goldberg
Yehudi Menuhin (Child prodigy violinist)

Composers
Irving Berlin
Anton Bruckner
Felix Mendelssohn
Wolfgang Amadeus Mozart
Francis Poulenc

Educators
Fred Terman (President of Stanford University)
William Samuel Johnson (President of Columbia University)
Frank Vandiver (President of Texas A&M University)
John Witherspoon (President of Princeton University)

Military leaders
John Barry (Senior Navy Officer)
Stonewall Jackson (Civil War General)
John Paul Jones (Father of the American Navy)
Robert E. Lee (Civil War General)
Douglas MacArthur (U.S. General)
George Patton (U.S. General)
Matthew Perry (naval officer who opened up trade with Japan)
John Pershing (U.S. General)
David Dixon Porter (Civil War Admiral)

Inventors
Alexander Graham Bell
Thomas Edison
Cyrus McCormick
Orville Wright
Wilbur Wright

U.S. presidents
John Quincy Adams
William Henry Harrison
Thomas Jefferson

Abraham Lincoln
James Madison
Franklin Delano Roosevelt
Theodore Roosevelt
John Tyler
George Washington
Woodrow Wilson

Preachers and religious leaders

Moses
Joan of Arc
John the Baptist
William Cary
Jonathan Edwards
Phillip Melanchthon
Dwight L. Moody
John Newton
John Owen
Charles Wesley
John Wesley
Brigham Young

Scientists

George Washington Carver
Subrahmanyan Chandrasekhar (Nobel Prize winner, physics)
Pierre Curie
Albert Einstein
Blaise Pascal
Booker T. Washington

Statesmen

Konrad Adanauer
Winston Churchill
Benjamin Franklin
Patrick Henry
William Penn
Henry Clay

Constitutional Convention delegates

Benjamin Franklin (Inventor and Statesman; listed earlier)
Charles Pickney III (Governor of South Carolina)
George Clymer (U.S. Representative)
George Mason
George Washington (First President of the United States; listed earlier)
George Wythe (Justice of Virginia High Court)
James Madison (Fourth President of the US; listed earlier)
John Francis Mercer (U.S. Representative)
John Rutledge (Chief Justice of the US Supreme Court; listed earlier)
John Witherspoon (President of Princeton University; listed earlier)
Richard Basset (Governor of Delaware)
Richard D. Spaight (Governor of North Carolina)
William Blount (U.S. Senator)
William Few (U.S. Senator)
William Houston (Lawyer)
William Livingston (Governor of New Jersey)
William S. Johnson (President of Columbia C.)

U.S. Supreme Court Justices

John Jay
John Marshall
John Rutledge (Chief Justice)
Sandra Day O'Connor

Writers

Hans Christian Andersen
Pearl S. Buck
Agatha Christie
Noel Coward (Playwright)
Charles Dickens
Bret Harte

C. S. Lewis
Sean O'Casey
George Bernard Shaw
Mark Twain
Mercy Warren
Daniel Webster
Phillis Wheatley
Leo Tolstoy

Famous homeschool parents

Christopher Klicka (Attorney and Senior Counsel of Home School Legal Defense Association)
John Travolta
Kelly Preston (Actress, wife of John Travolta)
Len Munsil (Attorney and President of The Center for Arizona Policy)
Lisa Whelchel (Former actress, "The Facts of Life," now a pastor's wife and author)
Michael Card (Singer, songwriter)
Mike Farris (Lawyer and co-founder of Home School Legal Defense Association)
Mike Smith (Lawyer and co-founder of Home School Legal Defense Association)
Paul Overstreet (Musician, songwriter)
Robert Frost (Pulitzer Prize-winning poet)

Others

Abigail Adams (Wife of John Adams)
Clara Barton (Founder of the Red Cross)
John Burroughs (Naturalist)
Andrew Carnegie (Industrialist)
Charles Chaplin (Actor)
George Rogers Clark (Explorer)
Pierre DuPont
John Paul Jones (Father of the American Navy)
Tamara McKinney (World Cup Skier)
John Stuart Mill (Economist)
Charles Louis Montesquieu (Philosopher)

Florence Nightingale (Nurse)
Bill Ridell (Newspaperman)
George Rogers Clark (Explorer)
Will Rogers (Humorist)
Jim Ryan (World Runner)
Andrei Sakharov (Nobel Prize winner, world peace)
Albert Schweitzer (Physician)
Martha Washington (Wife of George Washington)

Sources

www.home4schoolgear.com/
famoushomeschooler.html
www.homeschoolacademy.com/
FAMOUS%20HOMESCHOOLERS.htm
www.bridgewayacademy.com/
FAMOUS%20HOMESCHOOLERS.htm
www.homeschoolutah.org/pages/pastandpresent.htm
www.ahem.info/FamousHomeschoolers.htm

WORKS CITED

African American Homeschoolers Network. "Many African American Families Homeschool." Atlanta, GA: AAHN, www.aahnet.org/contact.htm, 2003.

Afrocentric Homeschoolers Association. Homepage. Ontario: geocities.com/blackhomeschool, 1996.

Bauman, Kurt J. "Home Schooling in the United States: Trends and Characteristics." *Working Paper Series* 51. Washington DC: US Census Bureau Population Division, 2001: 6-13.

Bielick, Stacey, Kathryn Chandler, and Steven Broughman. "Homeschooling in the United States: 1999." NCES Technical Report. Washington DC: US Department of Education, National Center for Education Statistics, 2001: 2001-033.

Bunday, Karl M. Learn in Freedom! Homepage. www.learninfreedom.org/socialization.html, 1999.

Burges, Eric. National Black Home Educators Resource Association. Baker, LA: NBHERA, www.nbhe.net, 2003.

Burton, Linda, Janet Dittmer, and Cheri Loveless. *What's a Smart Woman like you doing At Home?* Washington DC: Acropolis Books Ltd., 1986: 67.

Colfax, David and Micki. *Homeschooling for Excellence: How to Take Charge of Your Child's Education, and Why You Absolutely Must.* Victoria, Australia: Warner Books, 1988.

Cordes, Helen. "Battling for the heart and soul of home-schoolers." Salon.com Mothers Who Think, 2 Oct 2000: 1-2.

Danielson, Stentor. "Geographic Bee Champ: Michigan Ten-Year-Old." *National Geographic News,* 22 May 2002: 1-5.

Foster, Christine. "In a Class by Themselves." *Stanford Magazine*, Nov./Dec. 2000: 1-11. www.stanfordalumni.org/news/magazine/2000/novdec/articles/homeschooling.html.

Gray, John, Ph.D. *Children Are From Heaven.* New York: Harper Collins, 1999: xxiii, 95-97, 317.

Guterson, David. *Family Matters: Why Home Schooling Makes Sense.* New York: Harcourt Brace Jovanovich, 1992: 53-71.

Honawar, Vaishali. "National 'Bees' buzz with home schoolers." *The Washington Times,* 21 May 2002.

Jefferson, Rich. "Home schoolers win first, second, and third at National Spelling Bee." HSLDA Media Release. www.hslda.org/docs/news/hslda/200006010.asp, 1 Jun 2000.

Jonsson, Patrik. "The New Face of Homeschooling." *Christian Science Monitor*, www.csmonitor.com/2003/0429/p01s01-ussc.html, 29 Apr 2003: 2.

Levine, Beth. "Help Your Child Excel in School: Tips from Top Teachers." *Reader's Digest*, September, 1998: 145-50.

Clearinghouse on Educational Policy and Management, College of Education, University of Oregon, eric.uoregon.edu/publications/digests/digest151.html, September 2001.

Lines, Patricia M. "Homeschooling Comes of Age." *The Public Interest*. www.discovery.org/scripts/viewDB/index.php?command=view&id=277, 1 July 2000.

Llewellyn, Grace. *The Teenage Liberation Handbook: How to Quit School and Get a Real Life and Education*. Eugene, OR: Lowry House, 1998: 141-42.

Mason, Charlotte. *Home Education, Volume 1*. Quarryville, PA: Charlotte Mason Research & Supply, July 1993: 192-3.

National African-American Homeschoolers Alliance. Homepage. Chapel Hill, NC: ncaahomeschoolers. tripod.com/index.htm, 2003.

National Home Education Network. "Homeschool Soup." NHEN, www.nhen.org/media/default.asp?id=353, 2003.

National Home Education Research Institute. "Fact Sheet Ic." Salem, OR: NHERI, www.nheri.org/content/view/177/54/, 2001.

National Home Education Research Institute. "Fact Sheet IIe." Salem, OR: NHERI, www.nheri.org/content/view/178/57/, 2000.

National Home Education Research Institute. "Fact Sheet IIIc." Salem, OR: NHERI, www.nheri.org/content/view/179/55/, 2001.

National Home Education Research Institute. "Facts on Home Schooling." Salem, OR: NHERI, www.nheri.org/content/view/174/62/, 2003.

Native American Home School Association. Homepage. www.expage.com/page/nahomeschool2, 2003.

Native Americans for Home Education. Homepage. www.geocities.com/nuwahti/NAHE.html, 2003.

Ray, Brian D. *Home Schooling on the Threshold: A Survey of Research at the Dawn of the New Millennium*. Salem, OR: National Home Education Research Institute, 1999.

Ray, Brian D. *Strengths of their Own—Home Schoolers Across America*. Salem, OR: NHERI, 1997.

Reynolds, Dean. "Home Schoolers Strong Competitors in Spelling Bee." AbcNEWS.com, 29 May 2003: 1-2.

Rudner, Lawrence M. "Home Schooling Works!" HSLDA, www.hslda.org/docs/study/rudner1999/FullText.asp, 1999.

Sears, William, M.D. and Martha, R.N. *The Baby Book*. New York: Little, Brown, and Co., 1993: 323.

Shyers, L. Edward, Ph.D. *Comparison of Social Adjustment Between Home and Traditionally Schooled Students*. Doctoral dissertation. Gainesville: University of Florida, 1992.

Smedley, Thomas C. "The Socialization of Homeschool Children." Master's thesis. Radford, VA: Radford University, 1992. Summarized in *Home School Researcher* 8 (3): 9-16.

Smith-Heavenrich, Sue. "Kids Hurting Kids: Bullies in the Schoolyard." *Mothering*, May/June 2001: 70-9.

St. Clair, Jane. "What Causes Bullies?" www.byparents-forparents.com, 2006.

Stewart, Lee. *Home Schooling*. Marble Hill, MO: NAPSAC Reproductions, 1990: 7, 12-16.

Taylor, John Wesley V, Ph.D. *Self Concept in Home-Schooling Children*. Doctoral dissertation. Michigan: Andrews University, 1986. Summarized in *Home School Researcher* Vol. 2, No. 2, June 1986: 2-8.

Thampy, George Abraham. "Home Schooling Spells Success." *Wall Street Journal*, 7 June 2000: A. 26.

Vernon, Jennifer. "Ten Students Advance to Geographic Bee Finals." *National Geographic News*, 20 May 2003: 1-6.

Vernon, Jennifer. "Washington State Eighth Grader Wins National Geographic Bee." *National Geographic News*, 21 May 2003: 1-4.

Wald, Johanna. "The Failure of Zero Tolerance." Salon.com Life, 29 August 2001.

Zeise, Ann. "A to Z Home's Cool Homeschooling." www.gomilpitas.com/homeschooling/religion/religion.htm, 2005.

OTHER BIBLIOGRAPHY

Bunday, Karl M. "Socialization: A Great Reason Not to Go to School." Learn in Freedom! www.learninfreedom.org/socialization.html, 1999.

Eaton, Fran. "Home-Schoolers Must Respond to 'Big Media's' Guilt by Association Tactics." *The Illinois Leader,* 17 Nov 2003.

Farenga, Patrick. "A List of Selected Research on Homeschooling." Wakefield, MA: Holt Associates/ Growing Without Schooling, 1996.

Farenga, Patrick. "Homeschooling in the '90s: A Beginner's Guide to Learning at Home." *Mothering,* Fall 1996: 56-63.

Gatto, John Taylor. *An Underground History of American Education.* Oxford Village Press, 2001.

Gatto, John Taylor. *Dumbing Us Down: The Hidden Curriculum of Compulsory Schooling.* BC, Canada: New Society Publishers, 1992.

Holt, John. *Freedom and Beyond.* New York: E. P. Dutton & Co., Inc., 1972.

Holt, John. *How Children Fail.* New York: Perseus Books, 1982.

Holt, John. *How Children Learn*. New York: Dell Publishing Company, 1973.

Holt, John. *Learning All the Time*. Reading, MA: Addison-Wesley Publishing Co., Inc., 1989.

Holt, John. *Never Too Late*. New York: Perseus Books, 1991.

Holt, John. *Teach Your Own: A Hopeful Path for Education*. New York: Dell Publishing, 1981.

Holt, John. *What Do I Do Monday?* New York: Dell Publishing, 1970.

Kohn, Alfie. *No Contest: The Case Against Competition*. Boston: Houghton Mifflin Company, 1986.

Kohn, Alfie. *Punished by Rewards: The Trouble with Gold Stars, Incentive Plans, A's, Praise, and Other Bribes*. Boston: Houghton Mifflin Company, 1993.

Leistico, Agnes. *I Learn Better By Teaching Myself.* Cambridge, MA: Holt Associates, 1997.

Leistico, Agnes. *Still Teaching Ourselves*. Tonasket, WA: Home Education Press, 1995.

McDowell, Susan A., Ph.D. *But What About Socialization? Answering the Perpetual Home Schooling Question: A Review of the Literature*. Nashville: Philodeus Press, 2004.

Moore, Raymond and Dorothy. *Better Late than Early. Dutton Books, 1989.*

Moore, Raymond and Dorothy. *The Successful Homeschool Family Handbook. Nelson Books, 1994.*

National Association for the Education of Young Children. "Good Teaching Practices for Older Preschoolers and Kindergartners: A Position Statement of the National Association for the Education of Young Children." Washington DC: NAEYC, 1990.

Plent, Mac and Nancy. *An "A" in Life: Famous Homeschoolers.* Farmingdale, NJ: Unschoolers Network, 1999.

Sheffer, Susannah. *A Sense of Self: Listening to Homeschooled Adolescent Girls.* Portsmouth, NH: Boynton/Cook, 1997.

Sorokin, Ellen. "Home-schoolers start a new honor society." *The Washington Times*, 4 Jan 2003.

Index

221; life skills and, 224-225; social life and, 41, 83-85, 210-214, 210-214; spirituality and, 95-96

famous homeschoolers, 169, 217, 241-246

fashion, xvi, 136, 195. *See also* appearance; clothes/clothing

fathers, 17, 162. *See also* parents

field trips, 16, 48-50

fighting, 105. *See also* martial arts; violence

"fitting in," xvii, 34, 138, 175, 195

football games, 3, 122, 124, 178

4H, 16, 23

freedom, 117-128; as advantage of homeschooling, 28-29, 109, 124, 126, 173 (*see also* homeschooling, benefits/advantages of); to "be a kid," 8, 117-128; and community involvement, 185; as concern about homeschooling, 45-46, 72; and educational choice, 189; gaining, 104; and goal achievement, 179; homeschoolers' feelings about, 52, 62, 74, 79, 124, 171; homeschooling parents give kids, 90, 198; and learning, 62, 224; to make mistakes, 87-91; from parents, 75; for parents, 208-211, 214-215; and social settings, 69-70; and solitude, 69-70; and teens, 198; of thought, 198; to travel (*see* travel). *See also* independence

friends, 47-70; adults as, xi, 111, 140; community as source of, 41, 201; concern about homeschooling, xvii, 45-46, 59; family unity and, 210-214; goal of socialization?, 34; mixed-age, 49, 55-56, 63-69, 130, 172, 179, 189, 202; public-schooled, 194, 201; quality of, 53, 54, 57, 59, 62 (*see also* friendships, quality of); quantity of, 59-60, 134, 137; quantity of time with, 42, 49, 51, 53, 55, 124; spending time with in homeschool setting, 26-28, 49, 210-214. *See also* friendships; peers

friendships: forming, 184; parents having, 208, 209-210, 212-213; quality of, 49, 53, 54, 57, 59, 62, 70; strength of, 7, 49, 53, 59. *See also* friends; peers

fundamentalist homeschoolers, 152-153

gay/lesbian homeschooling parents, 160, 162

"geek," 133, 178

generation gap, xxvii

geography bee, national, 218

gifted children, 93-94

Girl Scouts. *See* Scouts

God, 95. *See also* Christ, Jesus; religion; spirituality

grades, 18, 118, 140-144, 180, 189-190

grandparents, 8, 15, 24, 119, 145, 212

Gray, John, 40, 103, 114, 146, 237

guidance, parental, 61, 103-104, 113-115, 149, 162, 224

guns, 41, 107

hierarchy, 134, 175-177

high school. *See* school, high

Hindu homeschoolers, 153

hobbies, 125

Holt, John, xiii, 103, 183, 237

homeschoolers, finding, 227-237, 238-239

homeschoolers, types of: adolescent, 8-9; adopted, 30; African American (*see* African American homeschoolers); African Canadian, 164; agnostic, 30, 162; Asian, 164; atheist, 30, 162, 164; Baptist, 164; biracial, 160; Buddhist, 153; Catholic, 153, 164; Christian, 30, 95, 153, 162 (*see also* groups, homeschooling: Christian); conservative, 152-153, 218; fundamentalist, 152-153; gay/lesbian, 160, 162; high-income, 31, 218; Hindu, 153; inter-faith, 162; Islamic, 153 (*see also* homeschoolers, types of: Muslim); Jehovah's Witness, 153; Jewish, 30, 95, 153, 162, 164; Latino, 153; Latter-Day Saints (*see* homeschoolers: Mormon); liberal, 218; low-income, 31, 218; Lutheran, 153; middle-class, 152-153; minority, 31; Mormon, 153, 228, 234; Muslim, 30, 95, 162 (*see also* homeschoolers, types of: Islamic); Native American, 95, 153; Native American Catholic, 153; non-religious, 30, 31; Pagan, 153; Presbyterian, 164; Quaker, 153; religious, 30, 31, 94; rural, 30, 218; secular, 20, 94, 234, 237, 238-239; Seventh-Day Adventist, 153; "special needs," 153; suburban, 30, 74; Unitarian Universalist, 153, 162; urban, 30, 218; vegan, 153. *See also* unschooling

homeschooling: adjusting/transition to, 239, 239-240; benefits of (*see* homeschooling, benefits/advantages of); defining, 12, 17-19, 219; growth of, 48; kids' feelings about, 136-138; personal choice and, 169; reasons for (*see* homeschooling, reasons for). *See also* unschooling; *and individual topics*

homeschooling, benefits/advantages of, 109-111; academics, xviii, 9; freedom/ time, 109-110, 124-127, 198; homework, freedom from, 110, 124-125; knowing self, 221; parent-child relationship, 111, 125; socialization, xviii, 11; spirituality, 95-96; travel, 110, 125, 126. *See also* homeschooling, reasons for; *and individual topics*